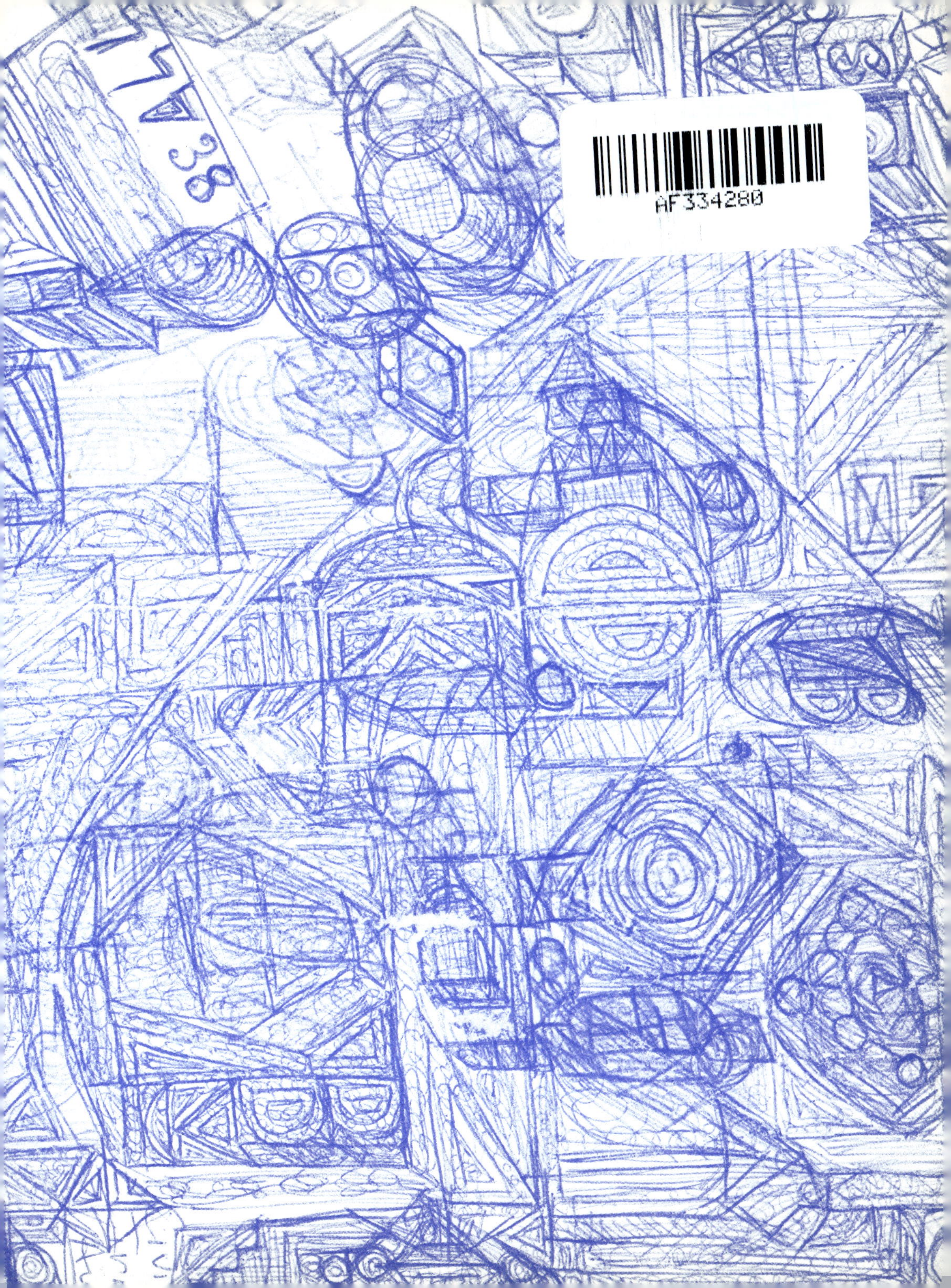

# Approaches to Drawing

Leo Walmsley

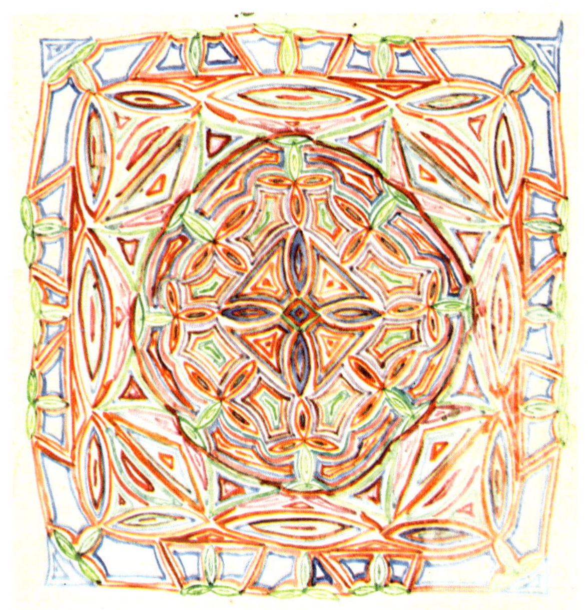

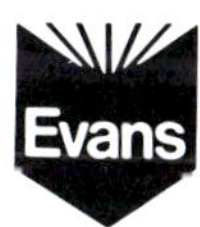

Evans Brothers Limited London

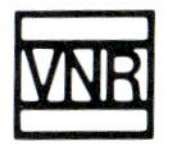

Van Nostrand Reinhold Company/New York

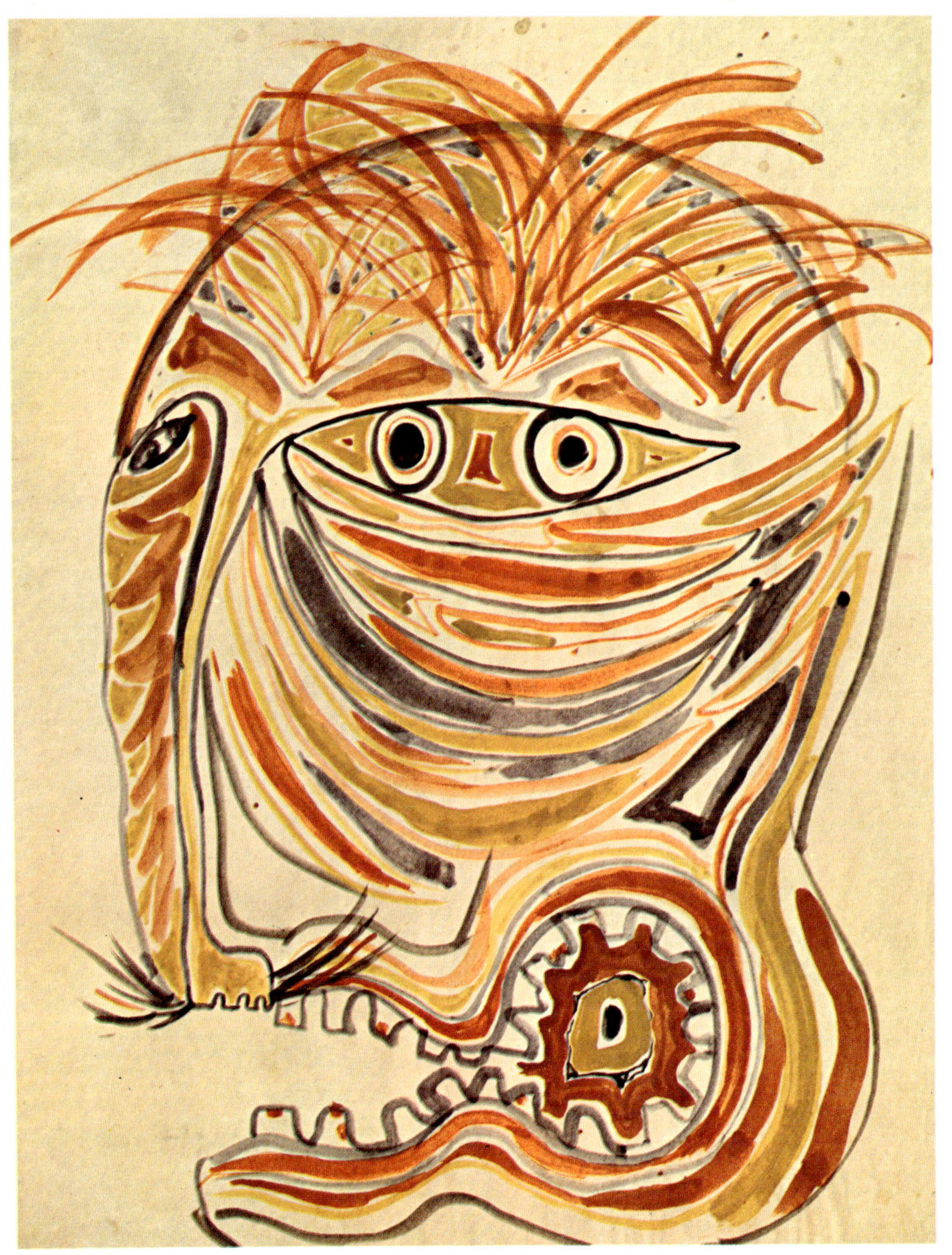

# Drawing is talking with shapes

Drawing is a quite normal and natural thing to do, and people have always been drawing for one reason or another. Everyone draws in some way every day. Even unconsciously, we doodle—which is drawing—on odd pieces of paper or on the blotter, the origin of the endpapers of this book.

Sometimes people draw for amusement, but most often for a serious reason. The first drawings which were made by Stone Age men—the cave drawings and paintings from the long ago of prehistory—were almost certainly thought up to improve the hunting, it being believed that making the image of something was a potent magic and gave power over what had been drawn or modelled. This belief is still held by some primitive, although intelligent, people. Those early drawings—often made in places very difficult to reach and far from the light of day—had a very serious purpose. They were not just Stone Age wallpaper to decorate the caves in which our remote ancestors lived.

We usually draw to tell other people something. It can be as simple and ordinary as a rough map showing the way to a house for a party. It may be a more complicated route map, drawn before printing, showing the village in the mountains where we are going for a holiday. It may be a way of describing the character of something seen, the materials from which it is made and the manner in which the pieces fit together —a steam engine, a house, a tree, the pebbles on the beach.

Drawing is an exciting activity, and drawings can show almost anything. Even without words. In fact the best drawings do not need any words at all. They show clearly what things look like, how they work, how different they are from other things. Drawings can even show what things feel like. Opposite is a drawing of a man with toothache. It does not try to describe a particular person as a camera would, showing the shape, colour and texture of hair and face, or a natural expression. It tries with its colours, dots, lines and shapes, to give an impression of the painfulness of toothache. Many artists throughout history have worked in this way to convey feeling rather than appearance.

**Drawing is making marks**

If you look closely at the 'toothache' drawing—and it is important to look very closely at everything—you will notice that it is made up of lines and other marks which make the shapes, either singly or together. All drawings are made up of dots and strokes and lines of many kinds which work together to produce the effect required.

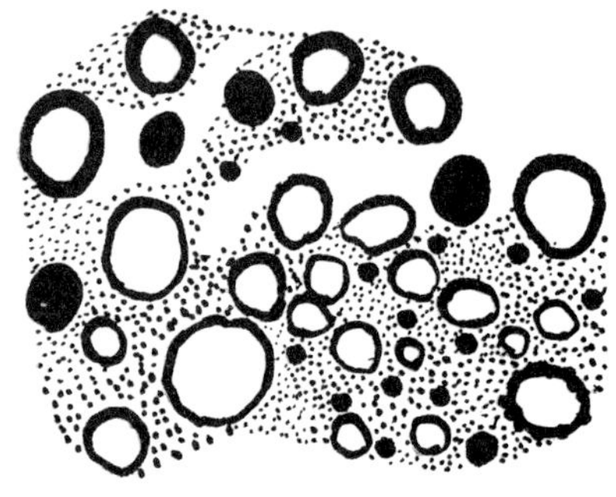

Here are more drawings. The first is just a simple pattern of dots and circles put together rather like plant cells viewed under a microscope. It was drawn by someone who did not think he could draw at all, but he can, as this interesting shape shows. The second is also a fine pattern of lines which says what a clock looks like when someone has overwound it, taken it out of its case, and been unable to put it together again. Then there is an owl printed after making marks in lino with a cutting tool. This is drawing also because many different tools and materials can be used to make drawing marks.

So whatever a drawing sets out to tell us, and whether it is simple or complicated, it is made up of marks of one sort or another. Marks which make shapes—small or large, regular or irregular, sometimes like something and sometimes not.

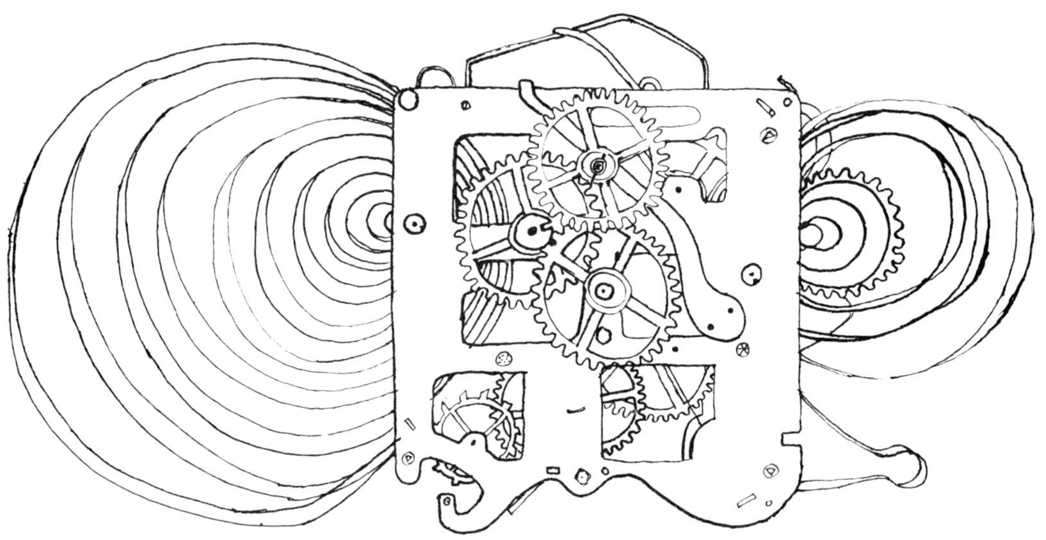

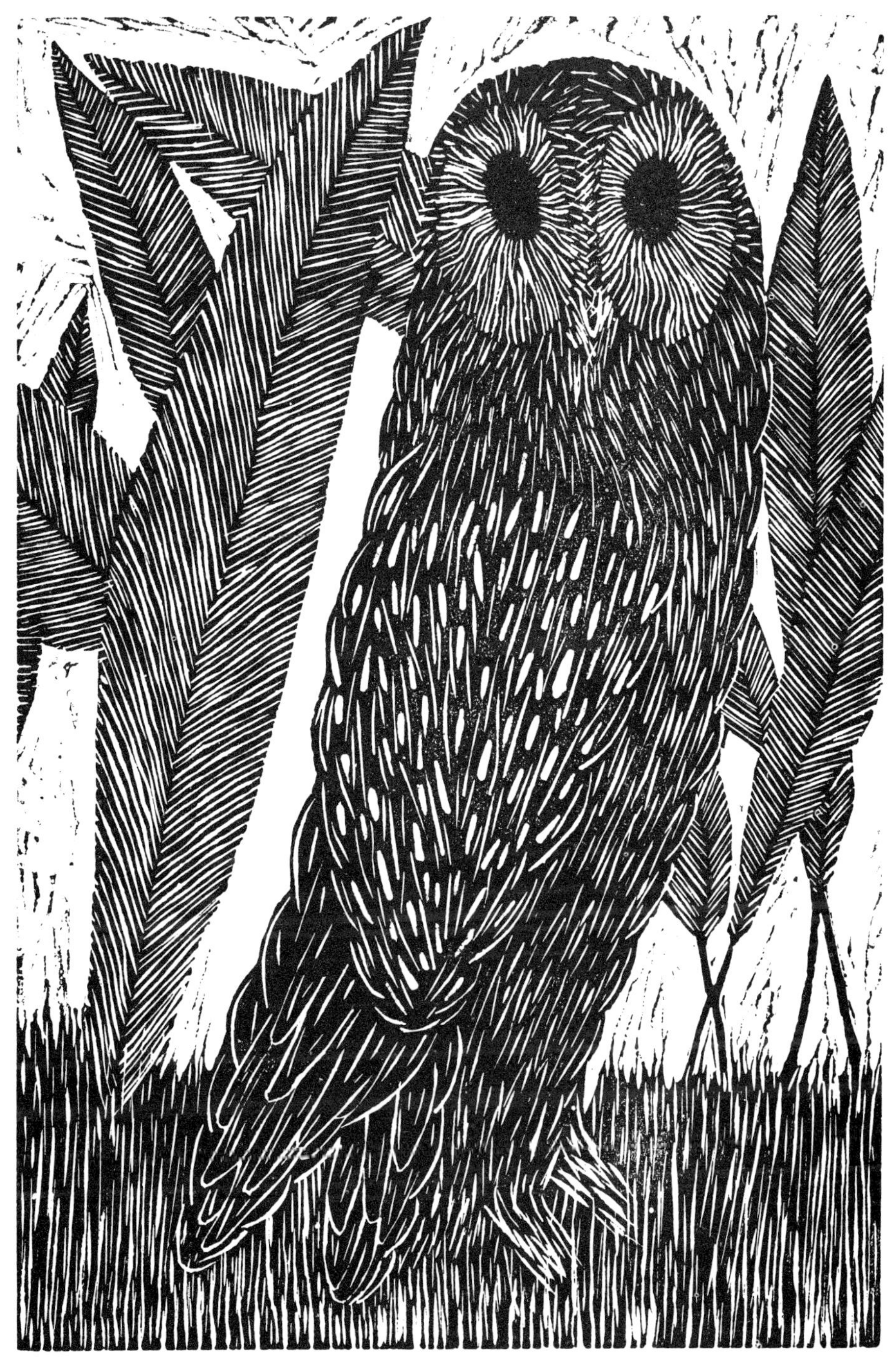

## Writing is drawing

Writing—and printing—is also made up of marks which make shapes. The marks are made in the same sort of way as in drawing, but they are put together into different patterns which have agreed meanings like CAT, COAT and COT. Early writing was exactly like drawing because the 'letters' and 'words' were made of pictures. Egyptian hieroglyphics show this clearly. Here is a letter and the separate marks it is made from:

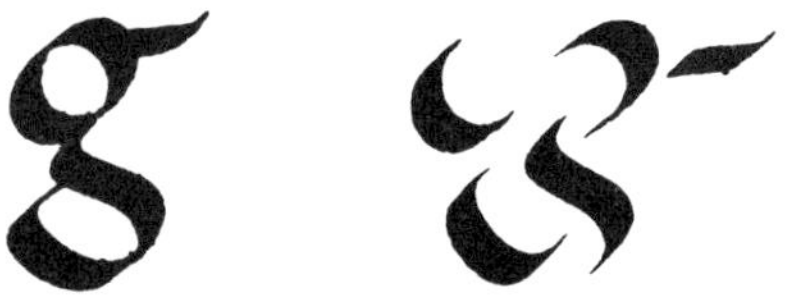

Observe its finely drawn shape.

Think of the twenty-six letters which you have been drawing for years. Those shapes, plus a few punctuation marks and figures, make up all the material we read—an enormous range from story books to free gift announcements on packages of cornflakes, comics, telephone directories, newspapers, signs and instructions of all kinds. Each letter shape originates as a drawn symbol. It is learnt by each of us, and flows from pen and pencil in drawn thoughts and messages every day.

Here is a pattern made from the letter C:

ccccccccccccccc

In the drawing below, although it is much reduced in size, it is still possible to see how many of the lines are made rather like writing in shape, or in a continuous rhythmic way. Opposite is a drawing which has been 'written' on to the paper in one line.

If you can write, you can most certainly draw.

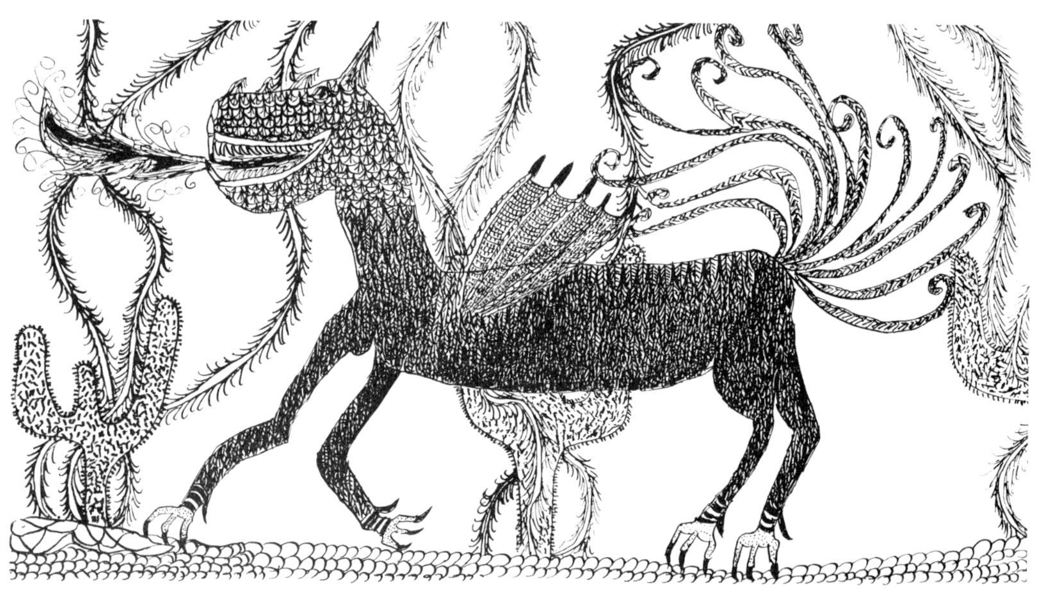

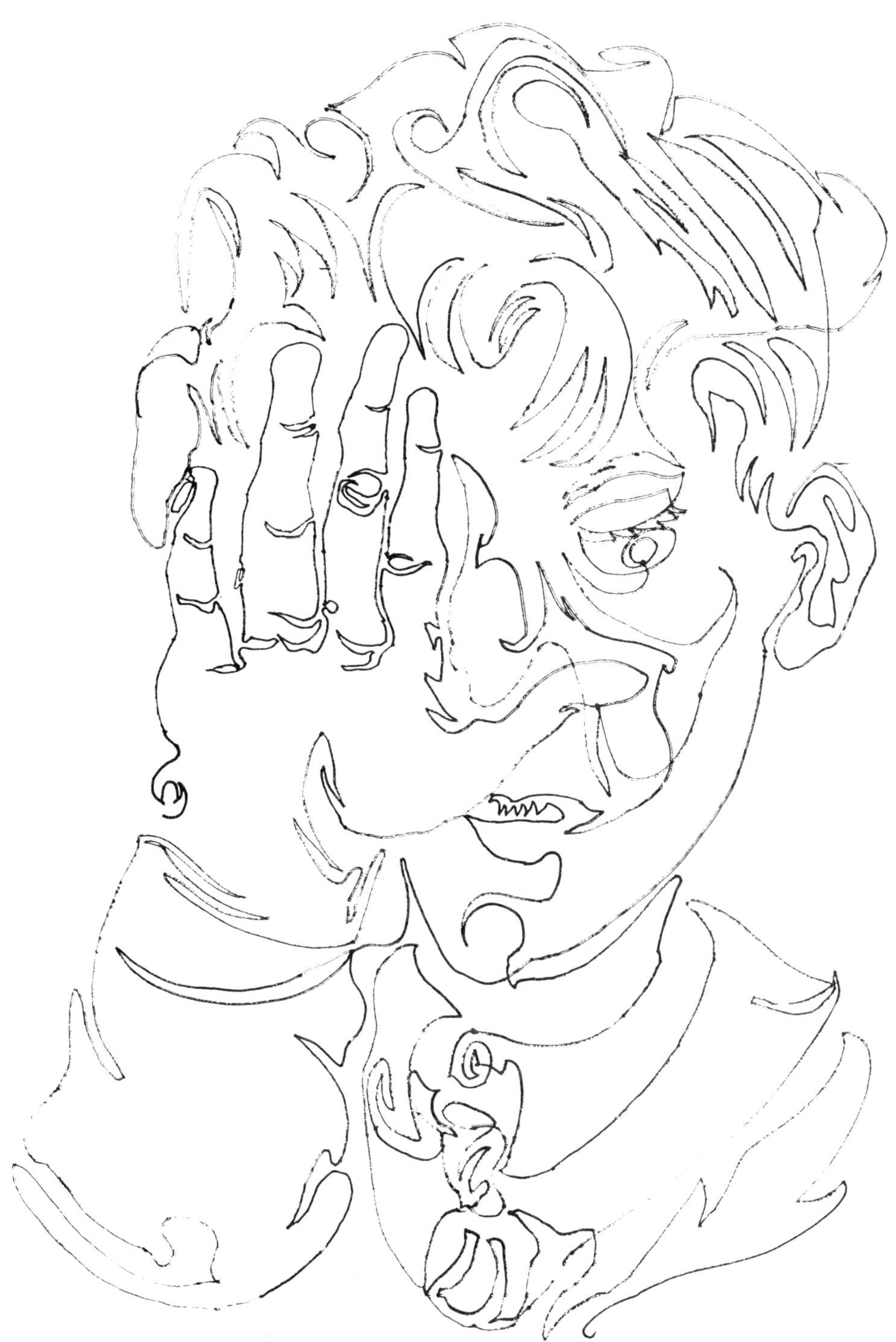

Thus, drawing, like writing, is a way of talking. In some ways drawing is a better method of 'speaking' than using words. Consider what this word says:

рыба

Now what does this drawing say?

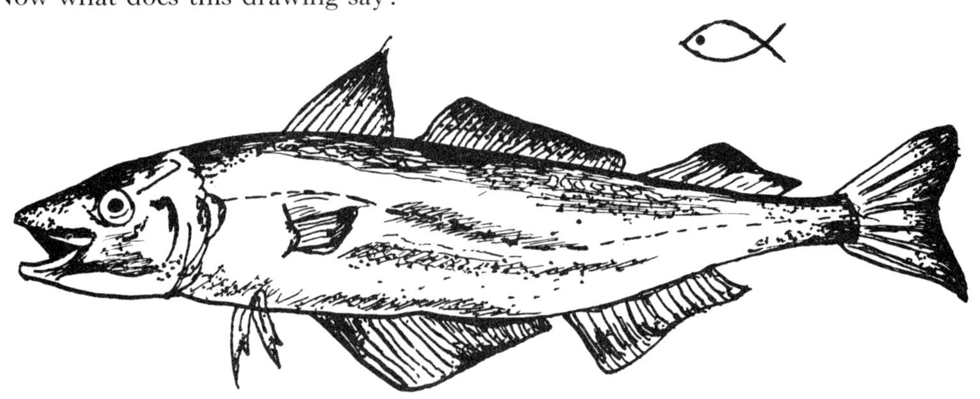

Unless you speak Russian the first pattern has no meaning although it is an interesting collection of shapes. The second pattern says 'fish' clearly to anyone who has ever seen one whether he is a Greek, Chinese or an Eskimo. Even the little fish symbol says 'fish' quite clearly.

Drawing is sometimes called a universal language. Its meaning is easily understood whatever word language is spoken or written. Road signs are such a universal language. They have to be!

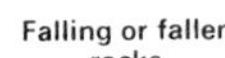
Falling or fallen rocks

Quayside or river bank

## Drawing is based on seeing

Seeing means looking very hard, very searchingly at everything. Those who look hardest at things usually draw better than those who do not. By looking harder, they see more, understand more,

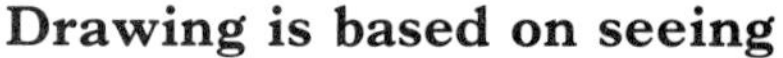

and have more to say. Such people can be said to be practised at seeing, and seeing properly does require a great deal of practice. There are some lucky people who are born geniuses and seem to make splendid drawings very easily, but most of us are good at things only because we work hard at them. Seeing and drawing are no more exceptions than cooking, boatbuilding or games.

So drawing is putting marks together to say something; it is based on looking hard at all the marvellous natural and man-made things of which the world is made, and—like everything else which we want to do well—it needs practice. To do it very well it needs a considerable amount.

Here is part of a Japanese woodcut. The drawing was made in wood with a knife, and the result was printed. It is not necessary to read Japanese to be able to understand it.

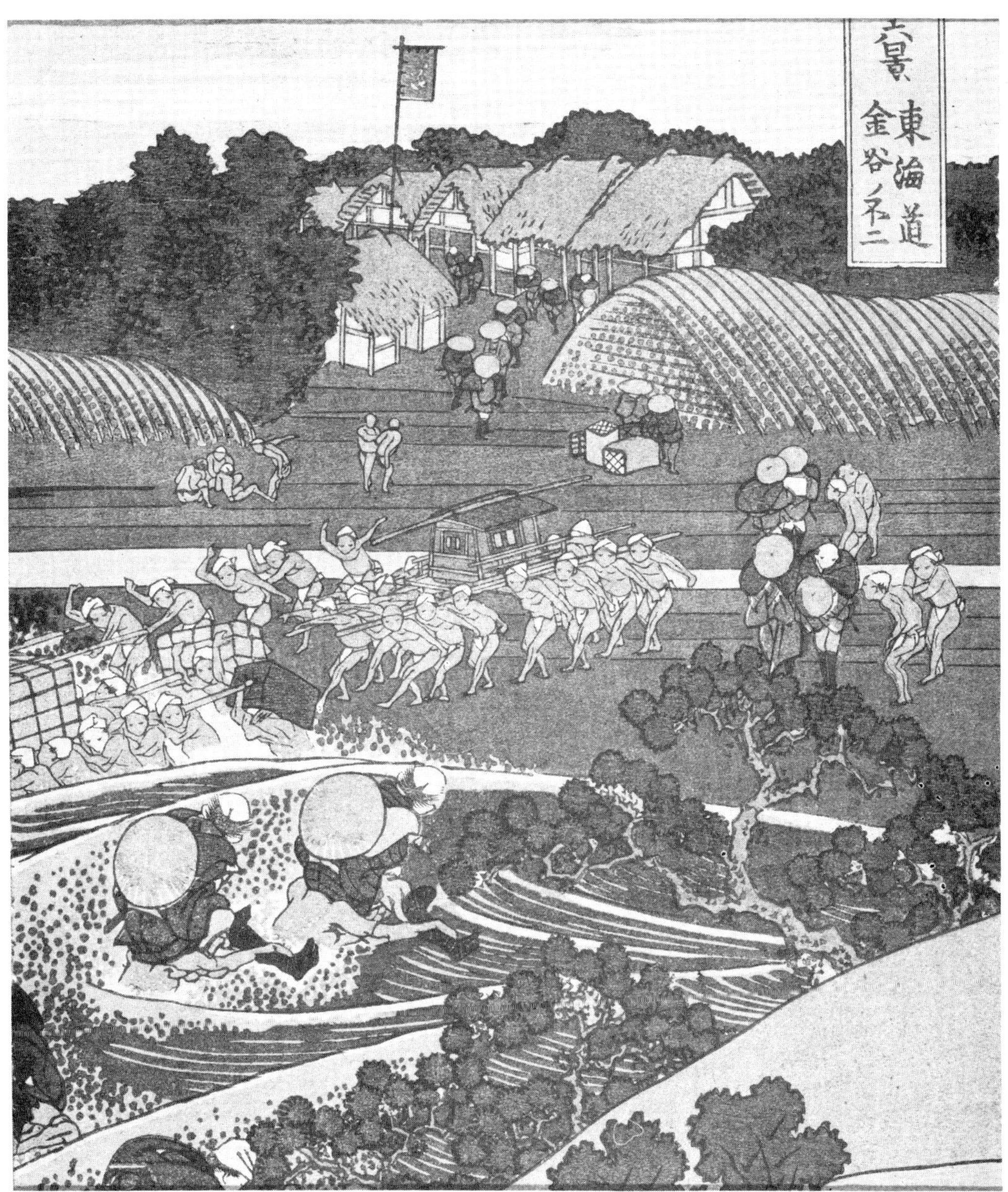

Look at something else, such as a fine old ship. Here is a photograph, but you should see real things when you can. Real things tell us more, and the best drawings grow usually from a real life experience like picking up a stone and seeing its curious shape, or wanting to make something and working it out on paper. Most made things begin with a drawing, whether a steam engine, a cathedral, a painting, a dress, a piece of jewellery or a teapot.

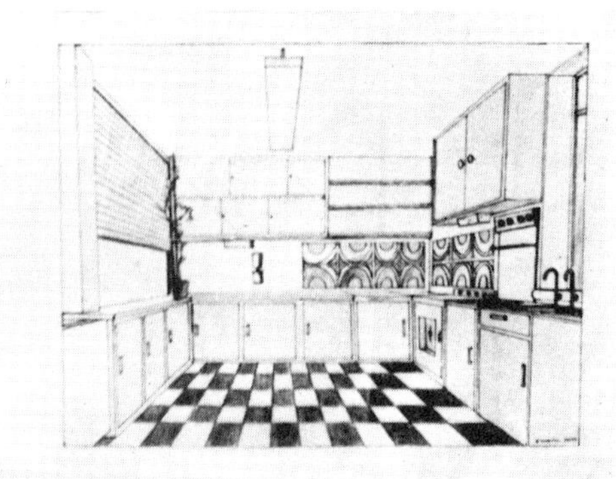

In this drawing an idea for modernising a kitchen was worked out before the expensive process of conversion was begun.

Drawing is a method of thinking, of asking ourselves questions and putting down the answers.

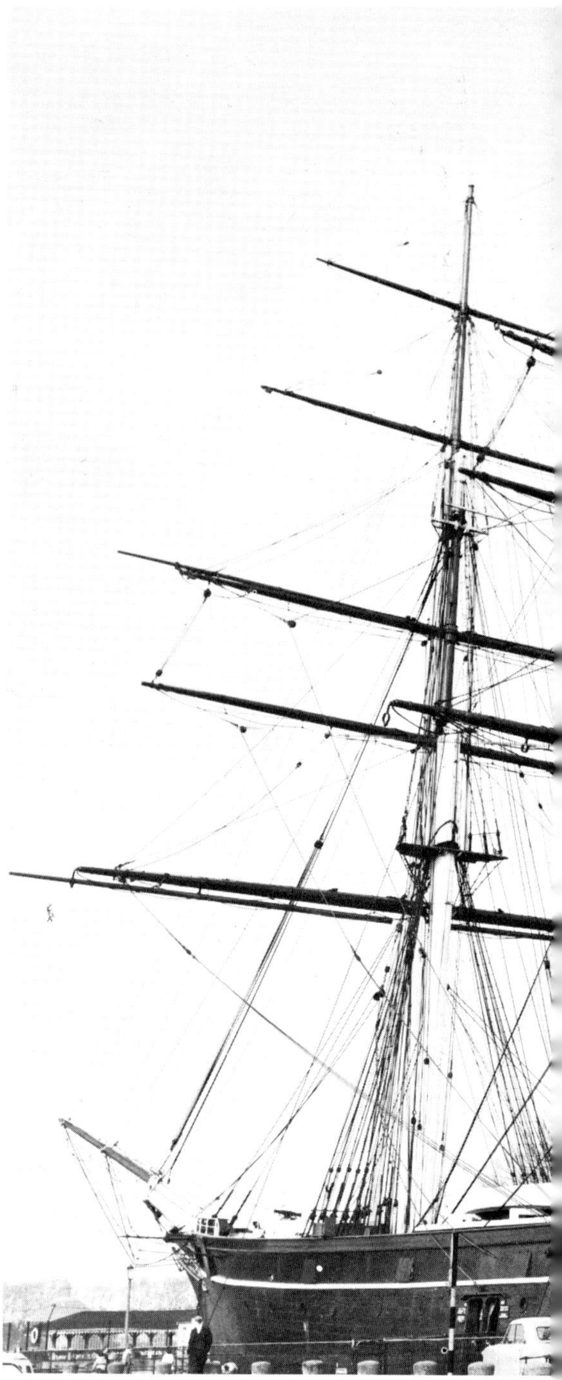

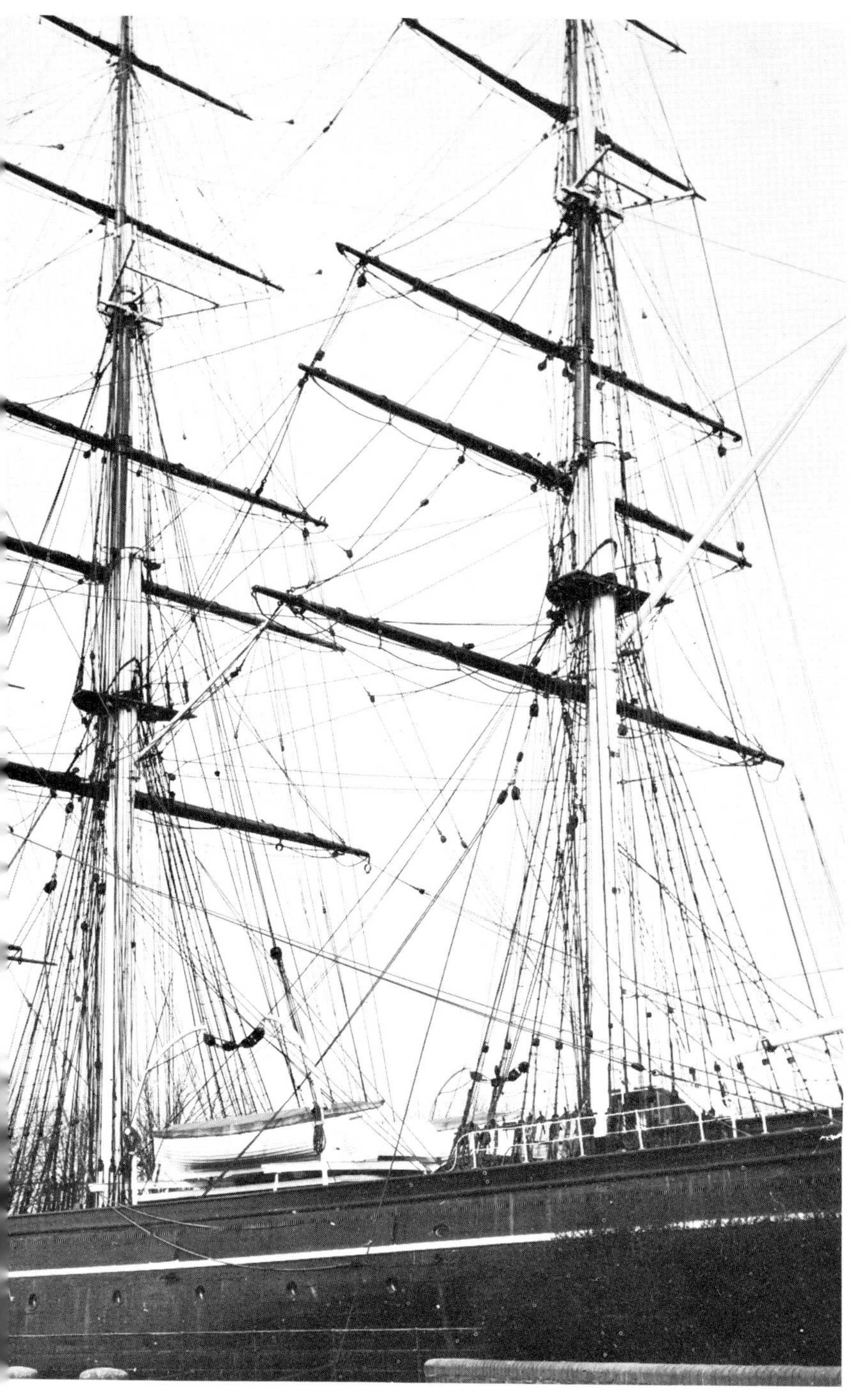

# Drawing is using lines

The photograph below shows how the masts and rigging of the *Cutty Sark* make a fascinating pattern of lines, some thick and some thin, and others in between. Many other real things are made up of 'lines' in this way, ranging from the delicate web of a spider to the massive structure of a girder bridge.

Drawing uses lines a great deal and it is said to be essentially linear. Let us look particularly at lines. First, opposite are some line arrangements in squares. These lines do not do anything except divide up the squares in different ways. You might try, and see in how many different ways you can do this. When drawing, YOU have to decide where the lines will go—not just hope that the pencil, or whatever is being used, will put them there. Each begins and ends at a decided point, and travels in a decided direction. This is good practice.

When you have tried dividing the squares, make a drawing which is rather more complicated, like the design opposite with its very careful deliberate line patterns. Of course, this can be done on a much larger scale. Drawing on different scales—even very big and very small—is also good practice as long as you choose the right medium with which to draw. The big drawings will make wall decorations and the small ones greeting cards.

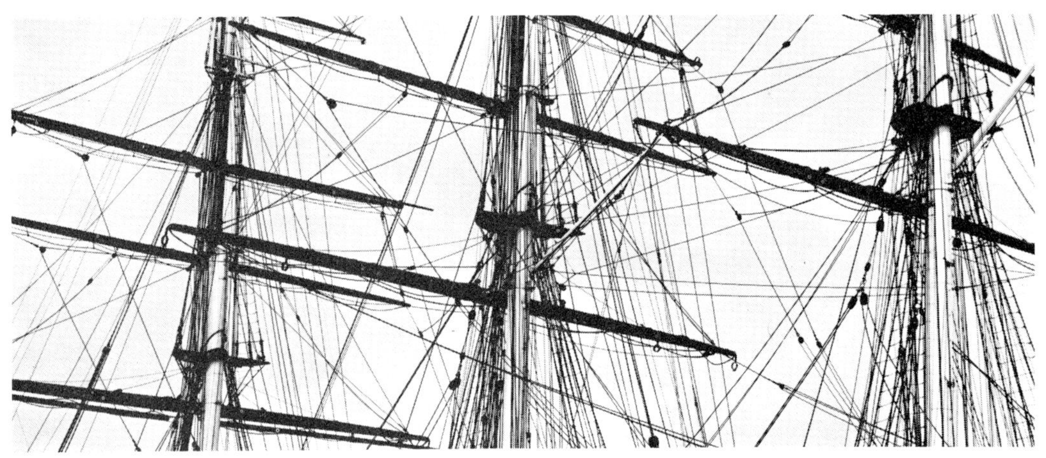

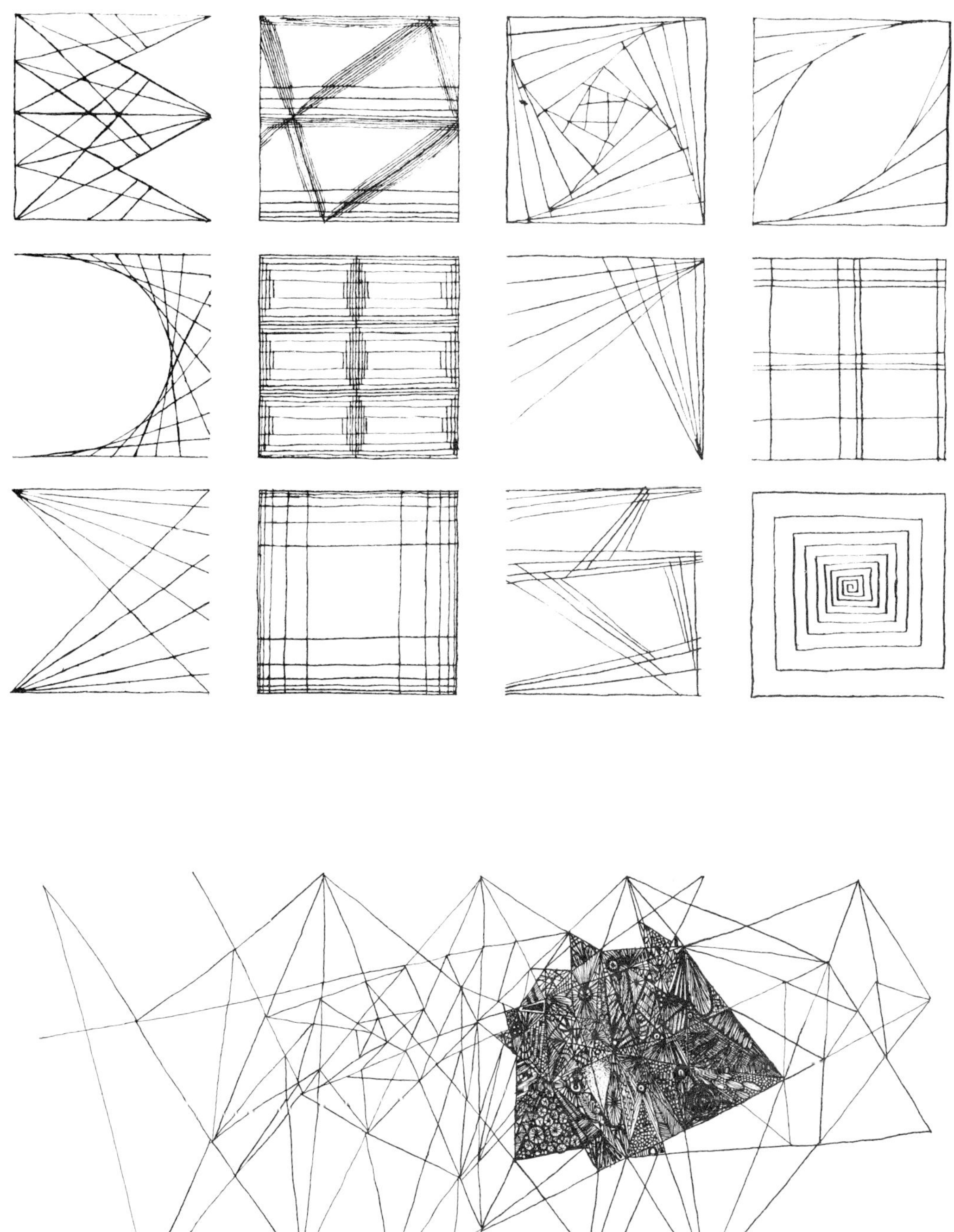

Before exploring the many different kinds of lines which can be made, look at the way in which lines can build up into a drawing of a 'real' thing. Take anything with a point which will make a mark and draw a line.

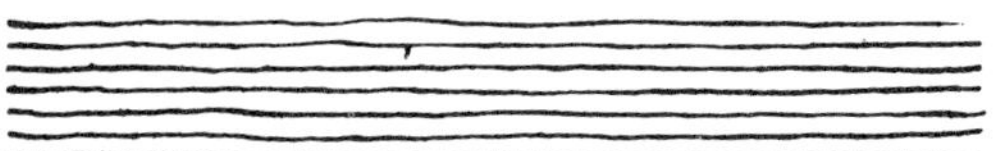

Now draw a number of lines in the same direction, trying hard to control the distance that they are apart.

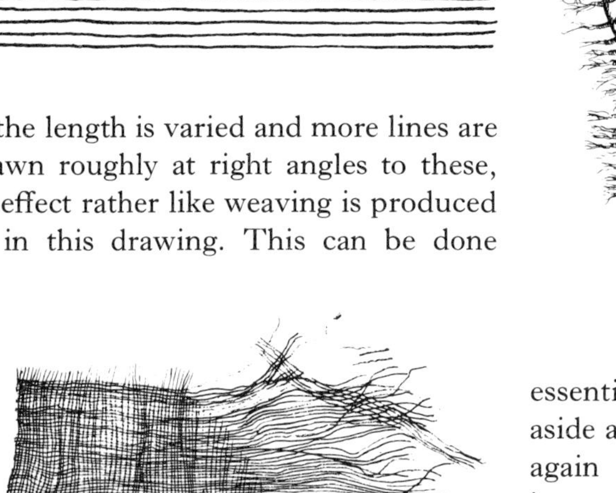

If the length is varied and more lines are drawn roughly at right angles to these, an effect rather like weaving is produced as in this drawing. This can be done

of a piece of rough sacking. It is not nearly as difficult as it may appear! But looking hard at the real thing first is

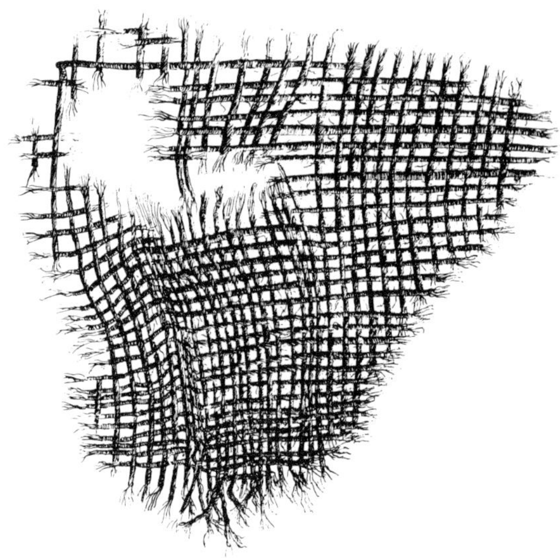

essential. See its pattern. Then put it aside and draw from memory. Look at it again after a time, and as experience increases, keep it in front of you all the time. In this way, the character of something is drawn and that is more important than drawing its exact appearance. If the direction of the lines is varied more, different effects will be obtained.

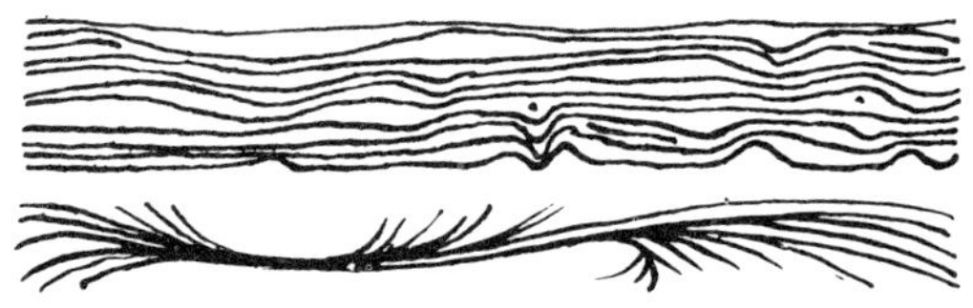

without much difficulty. You could go on to make a drawing similar to this one

That is how the piece of driftwood and the frayed rope opposite were drawn.

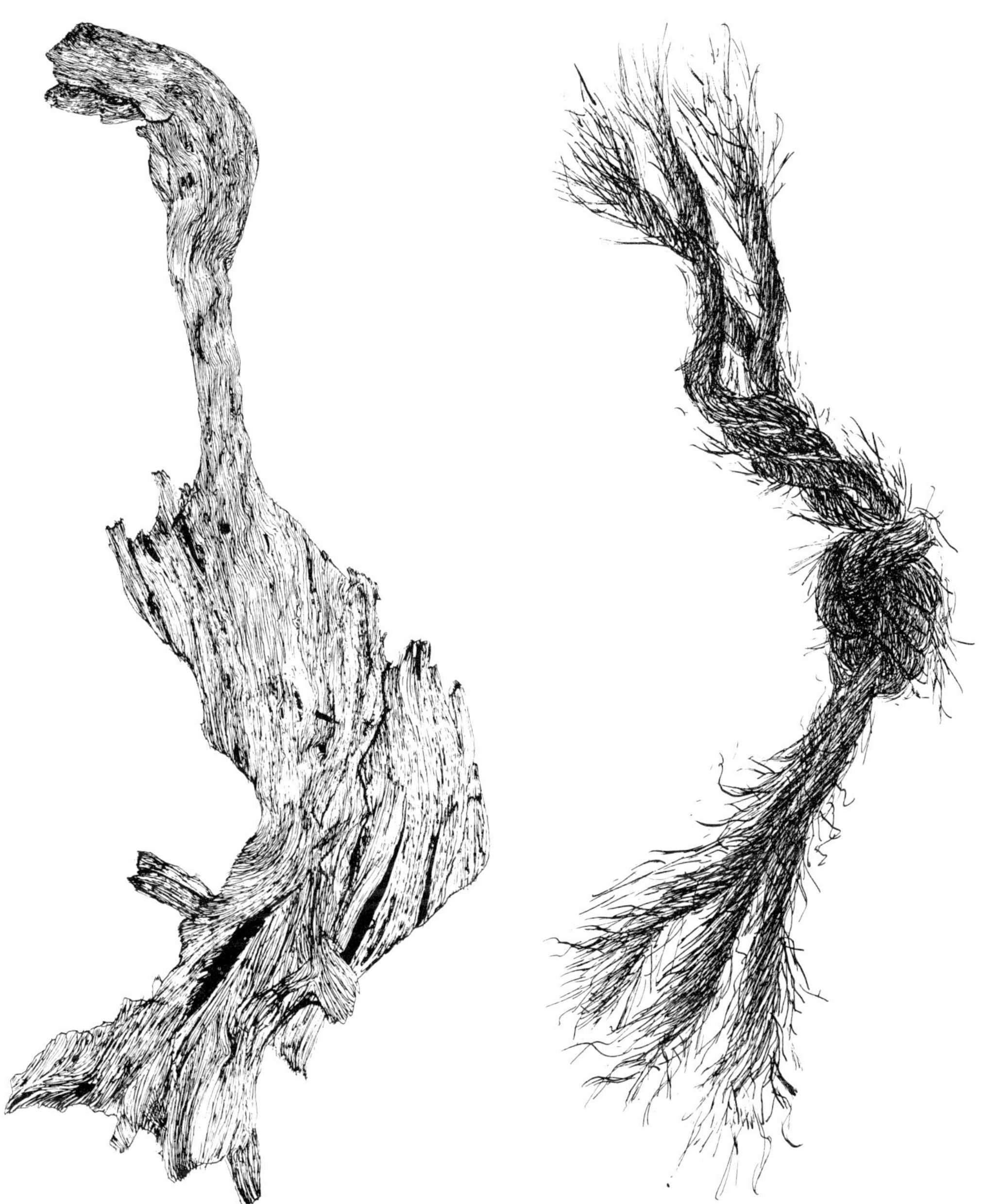

These drawings were much larger in the original, particularly the driftwood. This was a 'breakthrough' by a hesitant artist who had gained confidence in putting lines together.

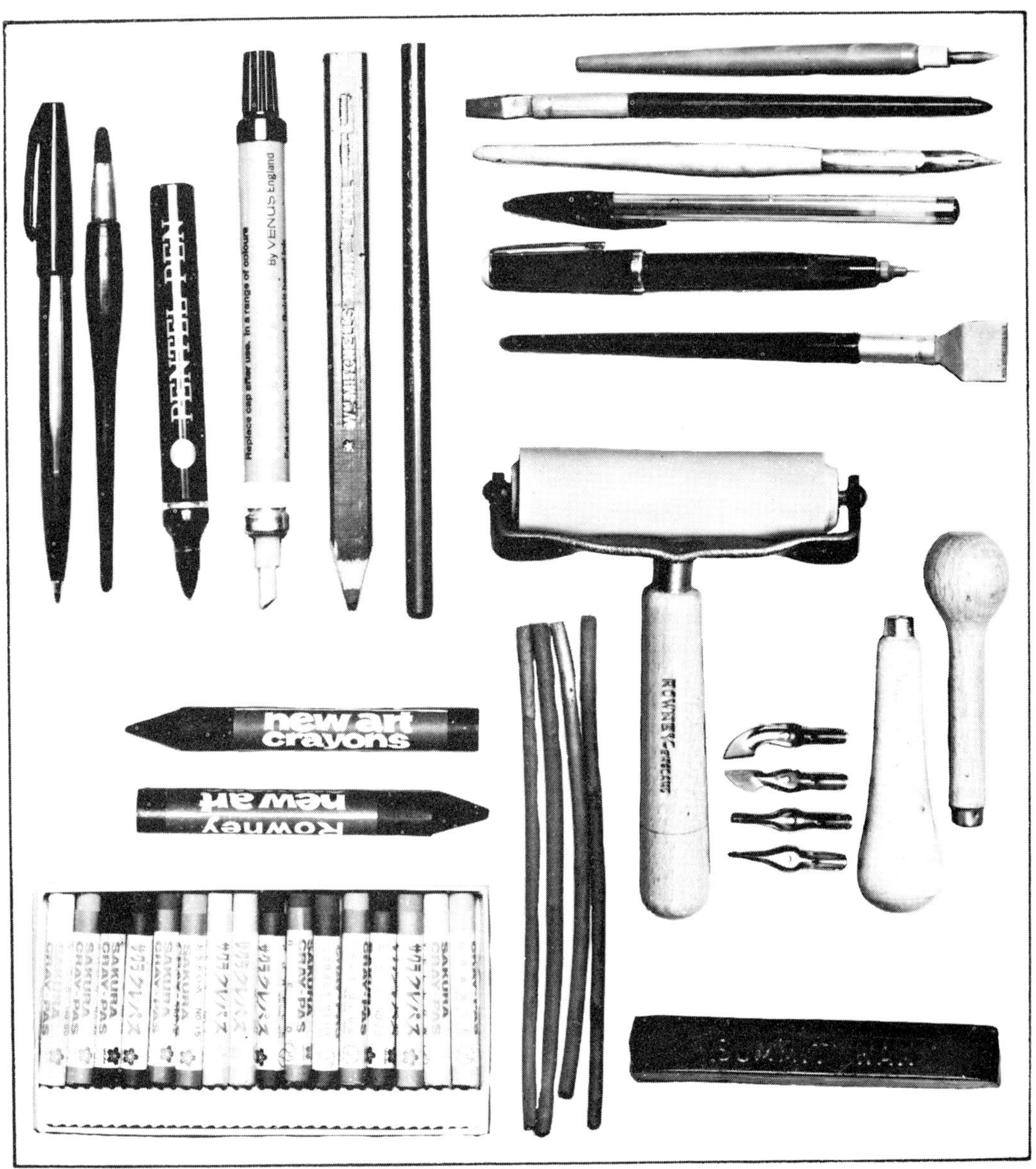

## Drawing tools

These tools with which to draw were bought in stationery and art shops. Each of them has its own particular character, and will make a large range of different marks. More exciting drawings will result from a knowledge of what each will do. They can then be exploited so that the most interesting and descriptive effects are produced.

The drawing instruments shown on this page were made at home. For most of your drawing the standard shop-bought pens, pencils, crayons, chalks and brushes will be used. They are convenient, clean and efficient and will make a very large number of different marks. But it is always interesting—and often desirable—to experiment with perhaps unusual materials. Some drawings may call for a range of marks which can be made more easily with home-made tools. Anything, of course, which will make a mark will serve for drawing. Even fingers. Almost certainly the first tools each of us used were our fingers.

Feathers of various sizes and types dipped in ink make versatile brushes. Pipe cleaners, tapered stumps made from rolled-up newspaper strips, used matchsticks—plain or chewed—straw, and cardboard strips are all very effective.

A whole range of pens may be made from pointed sticks, and especially good ones from thin bamboo and dried hollow plant stems. Cut these at an angle and sharpen them. They may be left unslit, or slit just like a bought pen, but the marks they produce are quite special. The traditional quill is formed in a similar manner from a suitably-sized feather. Other pens or brushes may be built from materials such as pieces of sponge, foam plastic, felt, or cardboard fitted into split sticks and tied with strong thread.

So many drawing tools are available, and

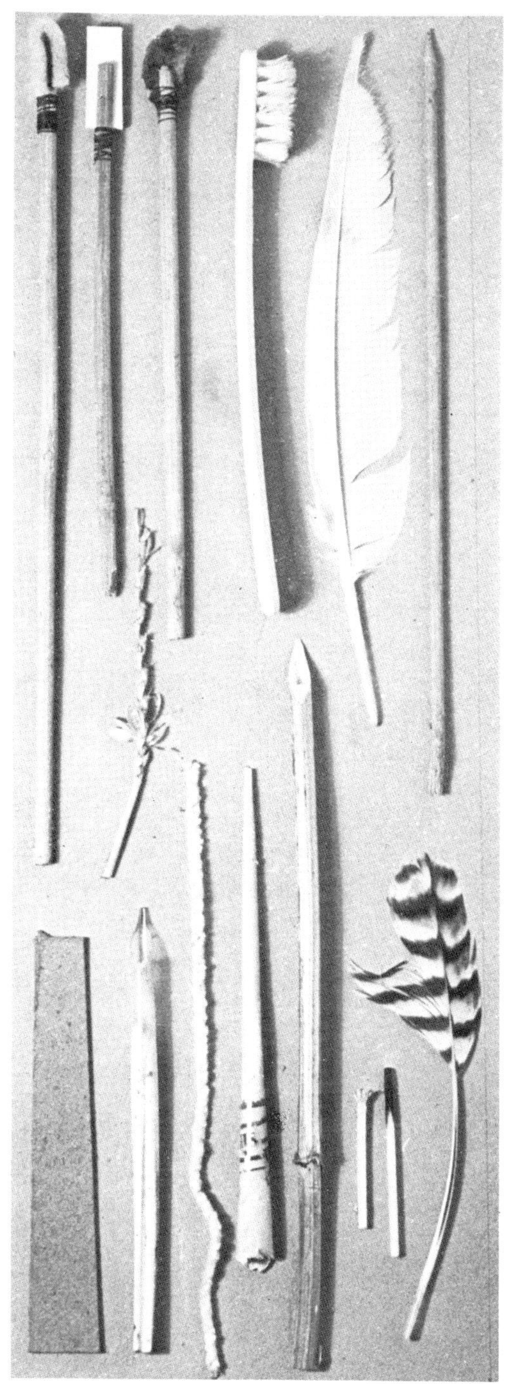

they may be hard, soft, crumbly, dry, wet, rough, smooth, greasy, pointed or blunt. As well as the obvious differences between pen and pencil and charcoal, between quill and sponge tip, each kind of tool may have differences. Pencils range in hardness and blackness from 9H to 6B through HB and F, each grade making its special family of marks. A pen may be very fine and hard, or fine and flexible (soft), or it may be large and coarse, wide or narrow. Other factors which will affect a drawing are the type of paper used and whether it is absorbent or not, hard or soft, dry, damp, rough or smooth. There are a surprising number of different types, from cheap newsprint to expensive hand-made papers for water-colour. The manner in which a drawing tool is held, pressed upon, and moved on the paper is most important. A soft pointed brush, filled with ink, will demonstrate this in a very effective way. Opposite are a few lines drawn with various tools—a broad carpenter's pencil, fine flexible pen, broad steel pen, felt tip, charcoal, chalk and a pointed brush. Try them yourself. Make up sheets of lines, exhausting what one tool will do before going on to the next. Those shown here are but a beginning of the endless range possible by varying tool, paper, pressure and manner of movement. The success of a drawing does depend very much on choosing the right tools and using them effectively.

Drawing is a process of finding out about things in more ways than one.

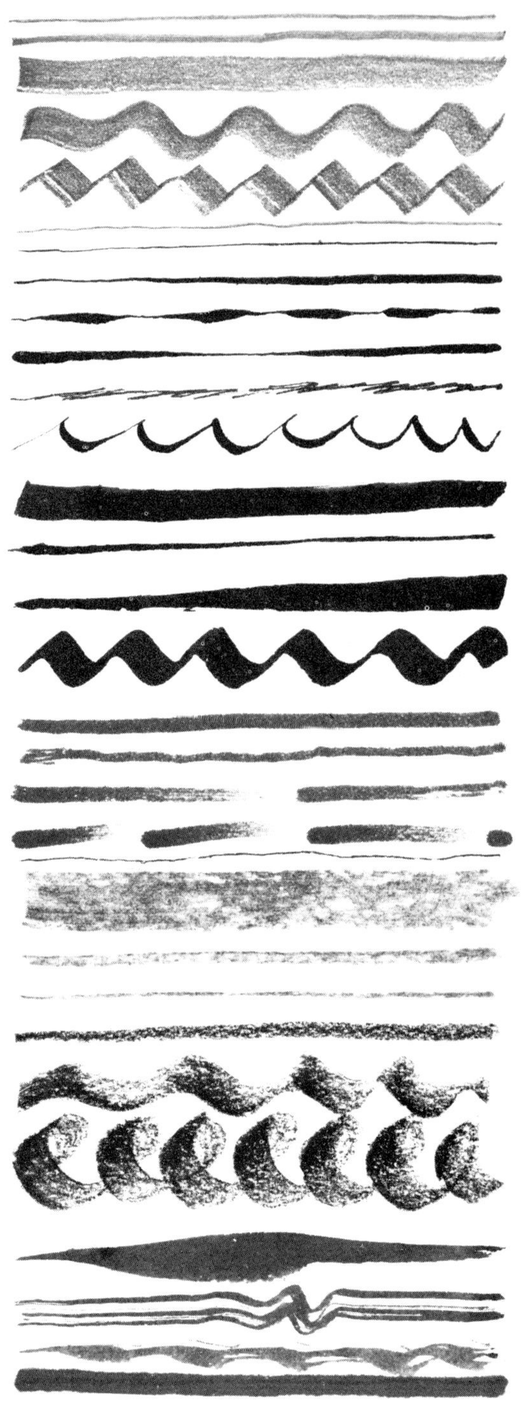

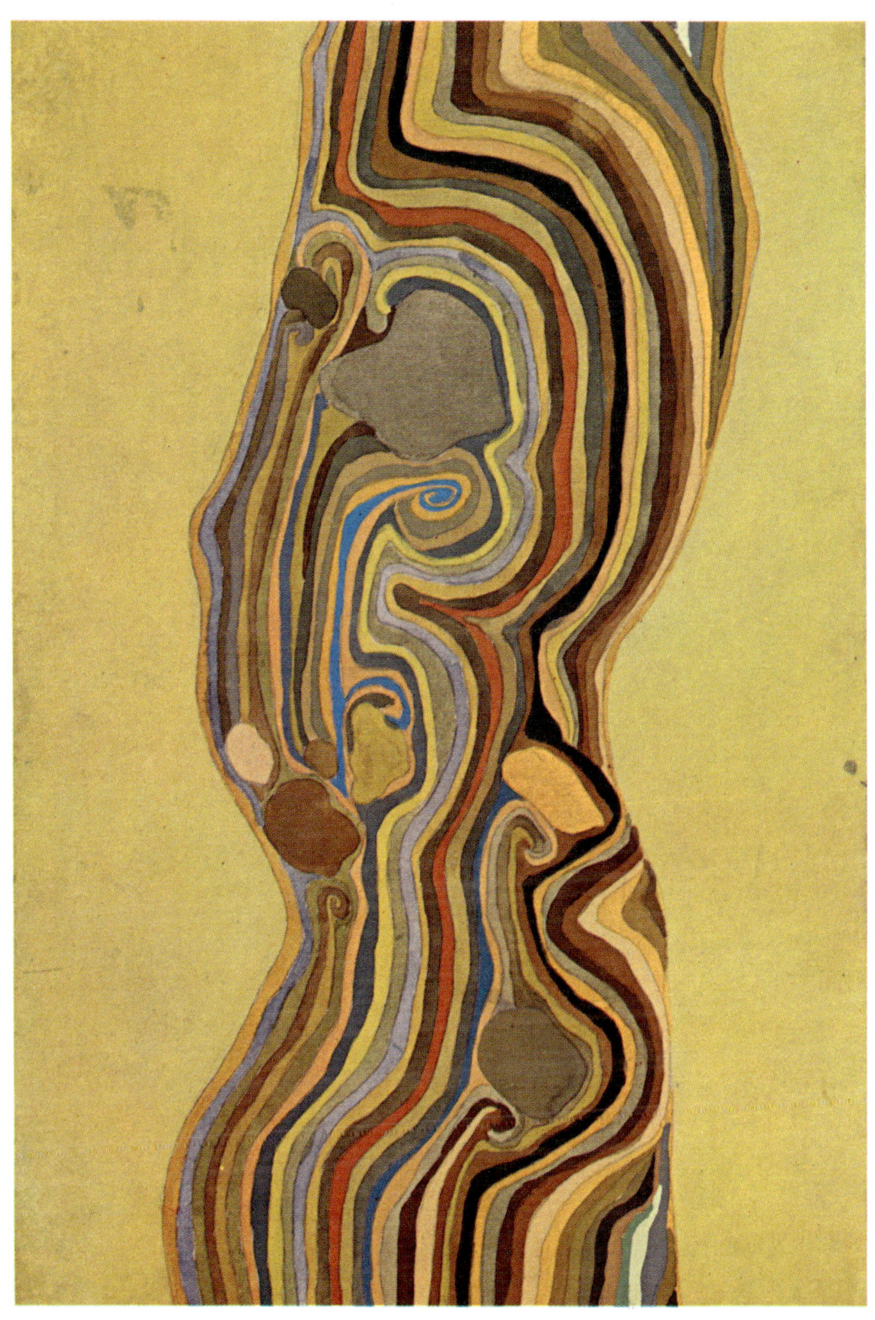

Lines with a brush moving round blobs.
The original is much bigger than the
drawings on page 15.

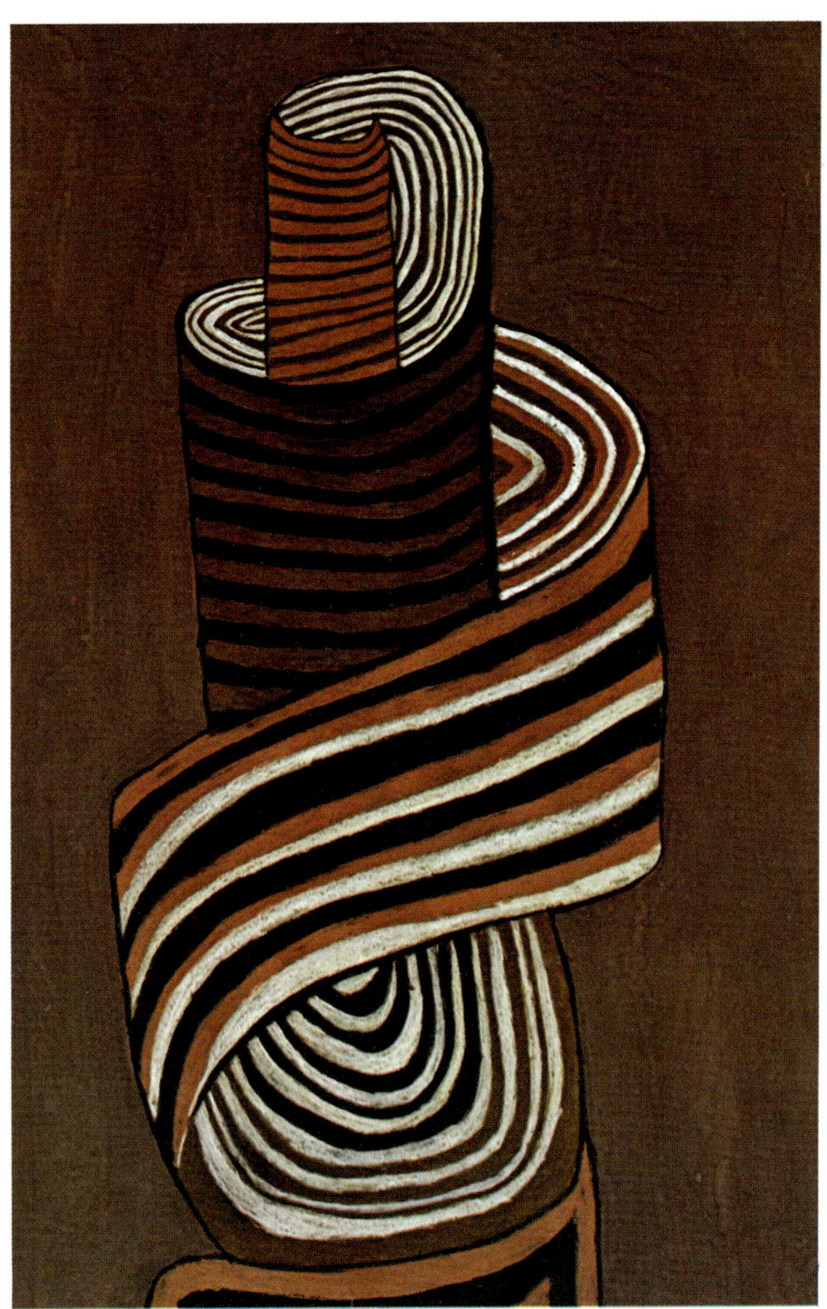

A very large drawing in pastel lines inspired
by a wood shaving.

## Lines are 'living' things

Make a spinning top from a disc of cardboard and a pointed stick—a spent match will do. Make an ink dot towards the outer edge and spin the disc. It will be seen that the dot becomes a line. All lines begin as dots, the first mark which is made when the drawing tool is brought into pressure contact with the paper. This is not noticed normally because the dot and its continuation into a line are made at once. Sometimes a dot is called a point, but most artists prefer to consider a point as a place where lines converge, meet or cross. The knowledge that a line is born as a dot, and a line is a dot which moves, is important in reminding us that a line is dynamic. It has energy: it has force: it has a life of its own. But it is the artist, of course, who gives it life! It is the artist who must take it on its energetic way, now fast, now slow, pulling, jerking, flowing, weaving, falling, rising; at one moment moving as delicately as a butterfly and at another thundering like a herd of buffalo, according to the feelings to be expressed and what other tasks the line has to do.

At the bottom of this page are three photographs showing how the same piece of black chalk will produce different lines with different finger movements. If you listen to a piece of music you will hear how the sound weaves and changes. Try drawing it!

We have seen how, as the medium is worked, a line is given direction and character; how, under control, it can divide a shape, describe a rhythm of growth in the grain of wood and the twisting of fibres. We have seen how it moves round the edges of a shape, shows how an object appears or is constructed; how a line can join with other marks to express feeling. These things can be done by arranging and varying the lines each tool will make.

A line can have the character of thickness or thinness, roughness or smoothness,

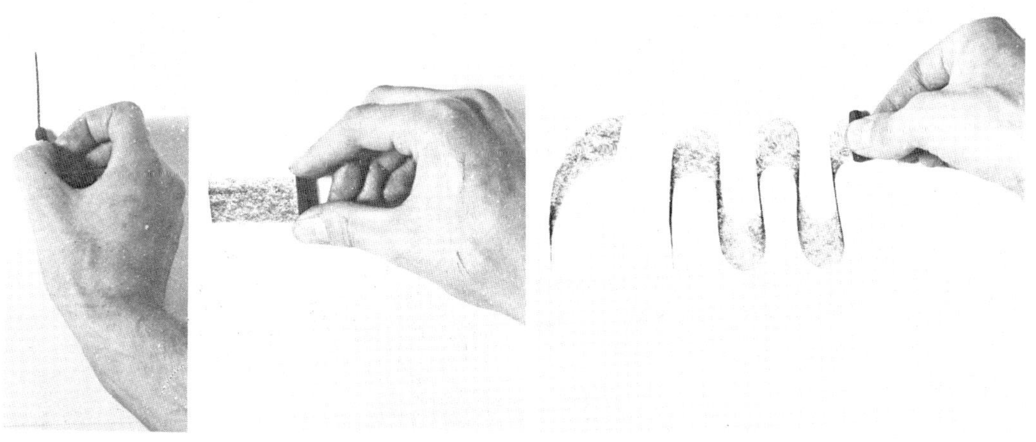

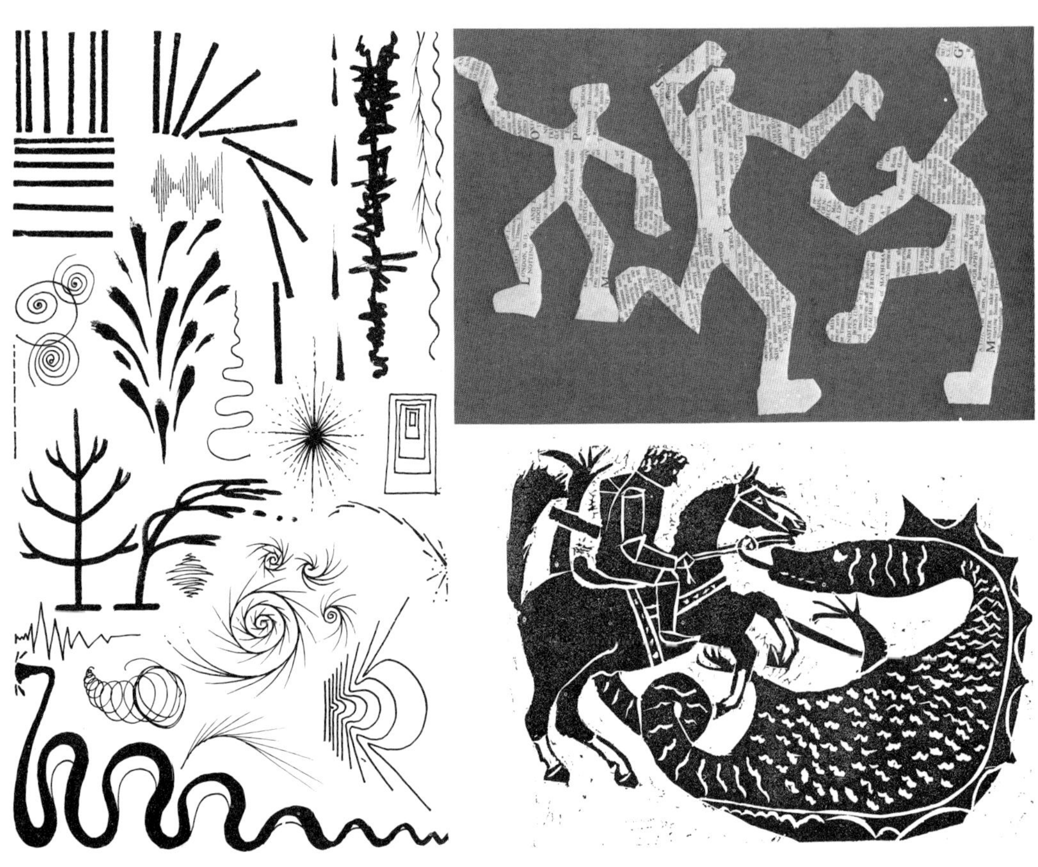

but it can also express a 'feeling' by the manner in which it moves. Lines can flow in a lyrical way or jerk in frantic movement, stand at rest or burst into violence, be in balance or fall over. Lines can expand and fret and crackle and fizz. They can move away from us or towards us. They can pile on top of one another to make surfaces which are rough as a coconut, or blend into the shine of polished steel. Lines move. Lines live.

Above 'are lines moving in different ways. Sometimes a whole drawing is a moving line as in the little cut-out figures and the linocut. All good drawings owe much of their vitality to the flow of the lines of which they are made and which emphasize mood or character.

You should experiment with moving lines, and shapes with linear movement. In doing so remember that lines are, in a sense, like people. At rest they stand (vertical) or lie down (horizontal) or sit (both). Thus vertical and horizontal lines show rest, calm, solidity, as in trees on a still day, unruffled water, or a building.

When lines move, like people they lean over, make curves and dash about. Like people they can be quiet, gay, restless and sometimes violent. Remember too, that as with the 'straightforward' lines on page 18 the way the tool is held and how it is moved, the amount of pressure used, and what the artist feels inside will make the line. It will never make itself.

Decisiveness is essential. If you are drawing a forceful jagged line, grit your teeth and feel forceful. If the drawing instrument breaks it will serve as a reminder that a forceful drawing demands a forceful instrument with which to draw. When drawing lyrical flowing lines try to feel lyrical. It would not be foolish to dance round the room first or listen to soft flowing music. Think of plants, and then draw plant shapes like those below. Not any particular plant, just something growing.

Draw pages of lines showing agitated and smooth movement, quietness and so on, each page with a different medium. It is often helpful to make a list of 'movement' words first. Or try drawing each sort of line with as many different tools as can be obtained or made. In this way it will be seen even more easily how a pen will produce a better spiky line than a soft crayon. What can be called our drawing vocabulary will grow stronger and stronger.

At this point it is worth attempting to draw a big picture from memory and imagination. The wind cannot be seen, but its effect can be shown in a simple landscape in the bending and twisting of the lines of grass and trees, the swirling of leaves, and perhaps by the leaning of people against its force. If a ship is drawn, like the *Cutty Sark*, battling through a storm, how should broken

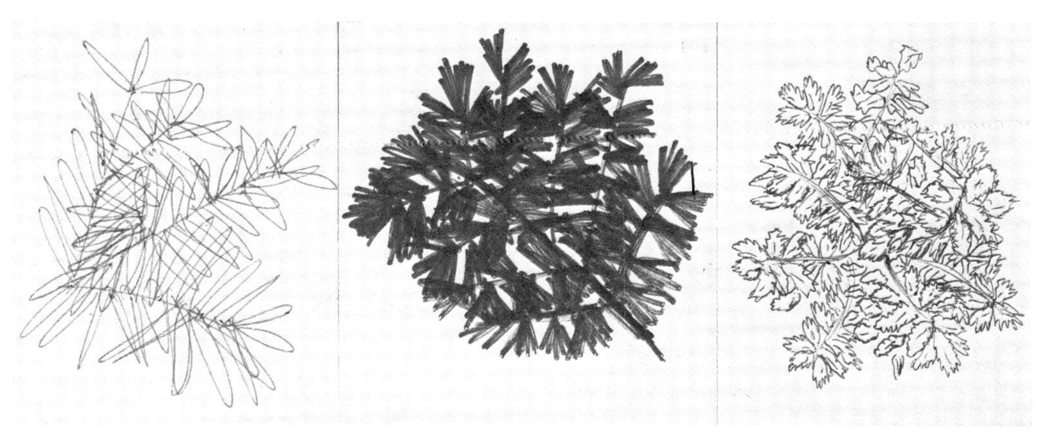

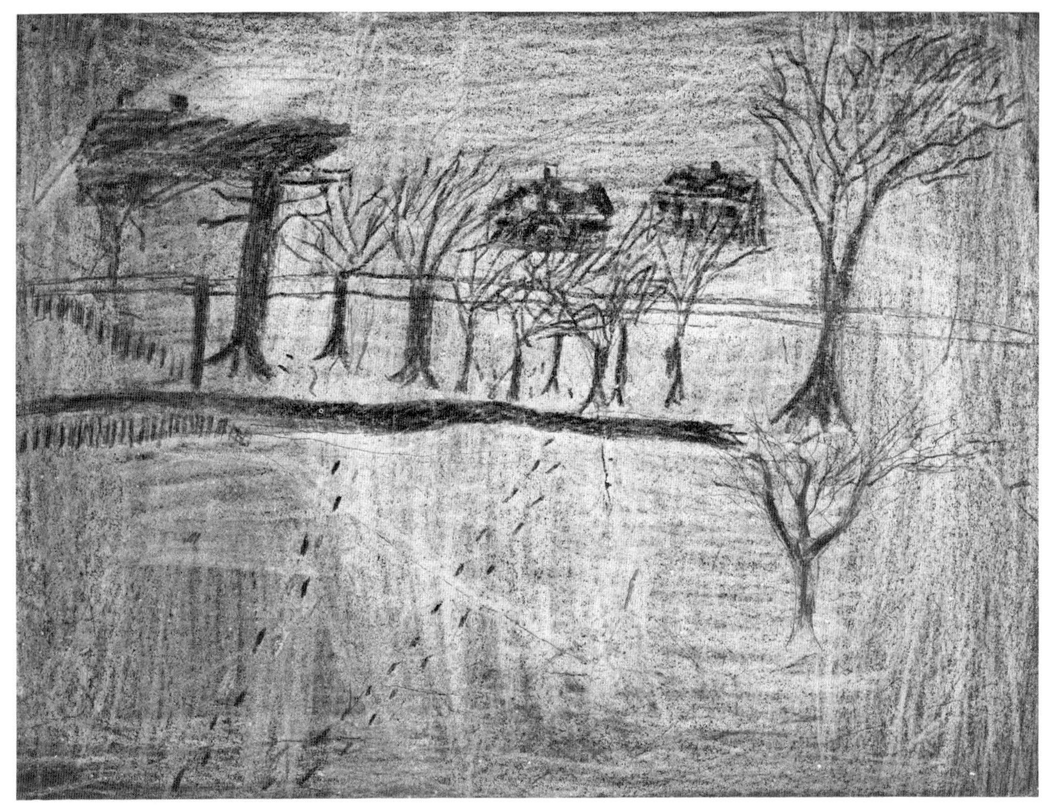

rigging streaming in the wind be shown? Or the lashing fury of the waves sending flurries of spray up into the straining yards? Is it better to draw with a crayon, or a brush or . . .?

The drawing above of a cold dark winter day was drawn on black paper with white and black crayon. The white crayon has been laid on the paper in line after line until they build up into the brightness in the sky and reflections on the snow-covered ground. The trees are still and winter-dead, black against the frozen earth and sky. Nothing moves. This frozen quiet is made by the medium chosen, and by the horizontal lines of hedge, fence and road, the vertical lines of the trees, and horizontal and vertical together in the buildings. Some variety and emphasis are given by the slanting lines of tracks, branches and the fence on the left. Notice also how the trees are spaced at different intervals Some variety is important to maintain interest, as in an appetizing well-balanced meal, but naturally, in a subject like this, too much would destroy the quiet mood.

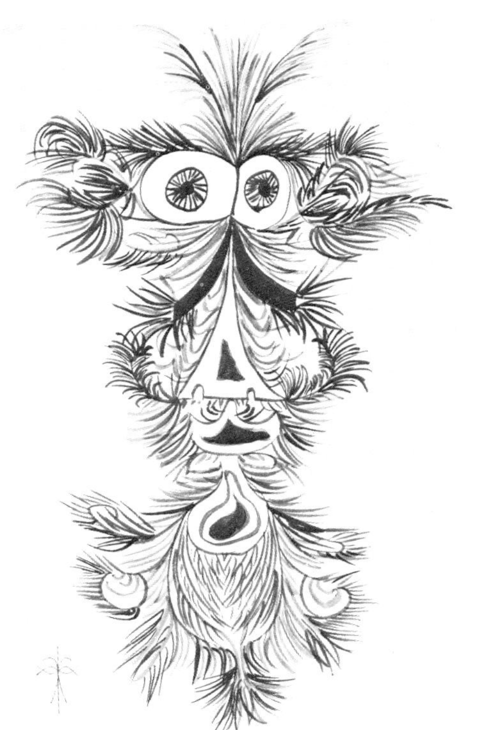

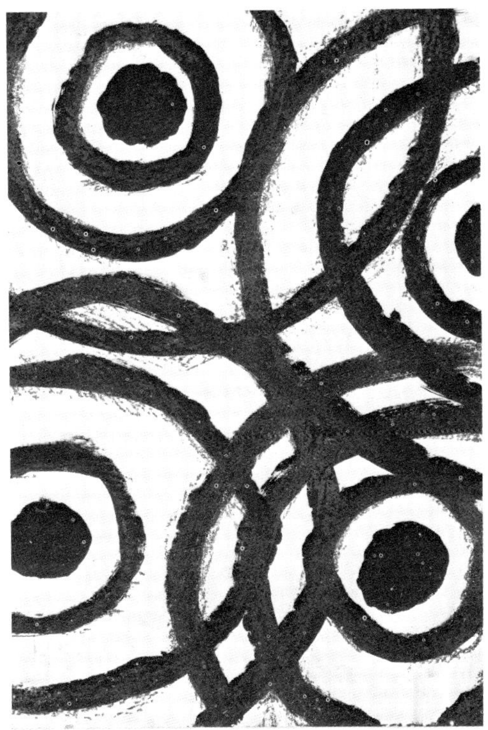

Making designs like the 'face' above is another way of experimenting with lines which grow. It was drawn with a soft pointed brush and the intention was to make lines of more or less the same thickness sprout from a central shape based on eyes, nose and mouth. This is an entertaining way of practising making lines grow out of each other—most important when drawing plants, figures and many other natural structures. It is also good practice for drawing faces. It is surprising how the main features of a face radiate lines, although usually not in as exaggerated a way as this! But as already observed, exaggeration for emphasis is often desirable. The little drawing in the corner shows the sort of skeleton with which a start can be made. It might be developed as a plant. Whatever the intention, it may be worked into a very complex drawing if you go on long enough.

The bold 'circles-in-a-pond' design was made with sweeping strokes using a candle on black paper. White paint was washed just over the edges of the candle strokes, which were then reinforced with black. It will be observed how forceful the movement is. These two designs show again the advantage of variety in approach. An adventurous desire to experiment pays dividends.

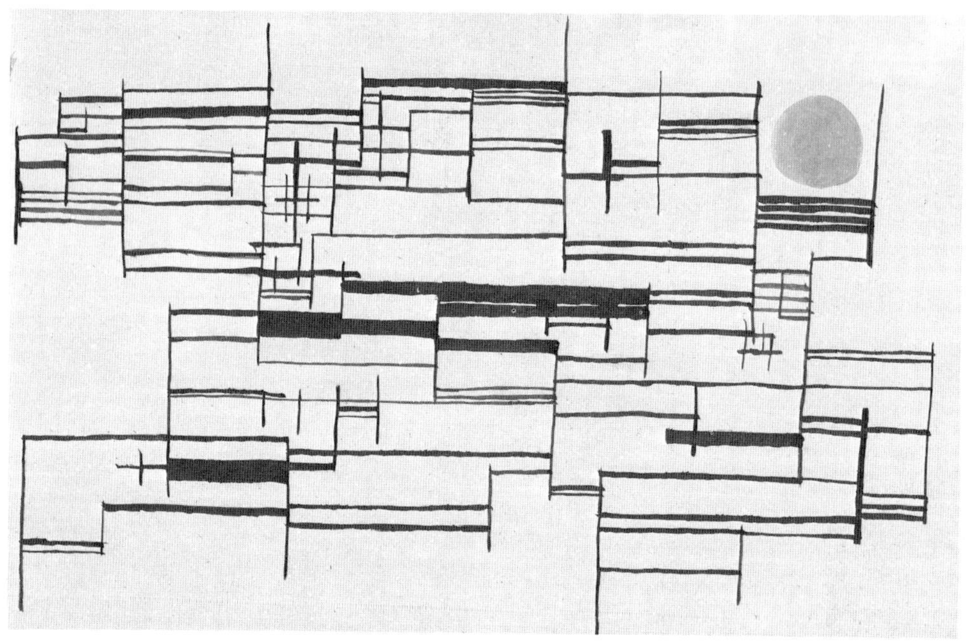

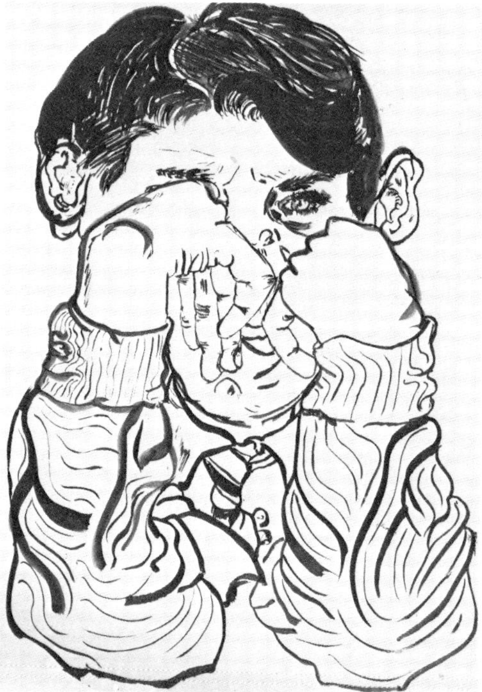

These forceful drawings have a character which is achieved in different ways. The restful lines of the 'townscape' above and the flowing movements of the lively figure below it grew from the exploring use with varying pressure of a soft hair

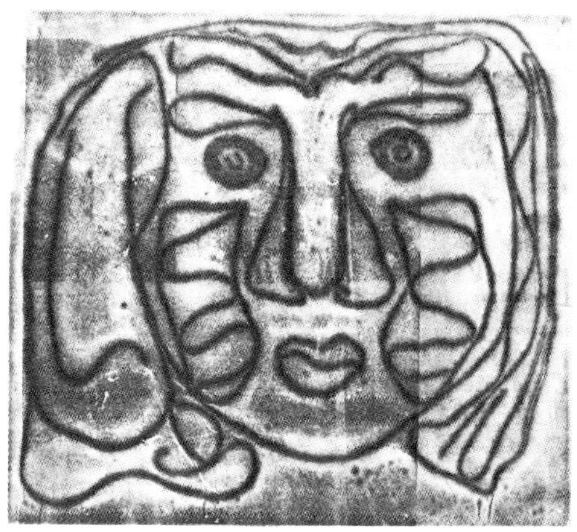

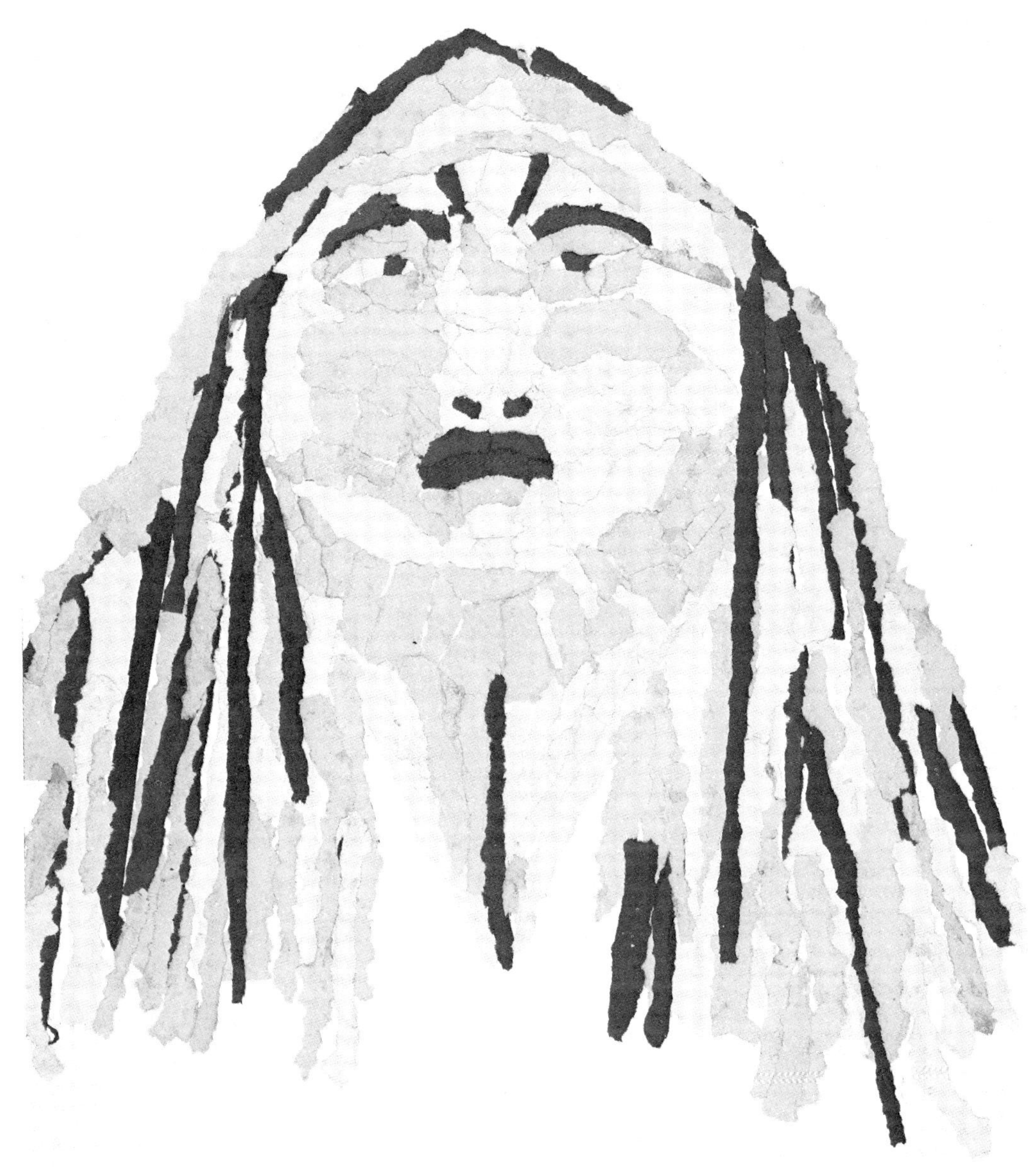

brush. The face on the left was printed from string laid on cardboard, the paper placed over the string and pressed with an inked roller. The drawing above was made from pieces of paper, the lines 'drawn' as the paper was torn. This technique will appear again when tone is considered.

This 'drawing' was made by cutting curved lines into paper shapes. These were laid on the backing paper and 'exploded' into the flowing swirling lines of the drawing, the pieces being stuck down as it was built up without drawing an outline. Some pieces were reversed or their positions changed, but it can be seen how many have just moved apart. A tiger drawn in this way is a rewarding experience and makes a fine decorative shape.

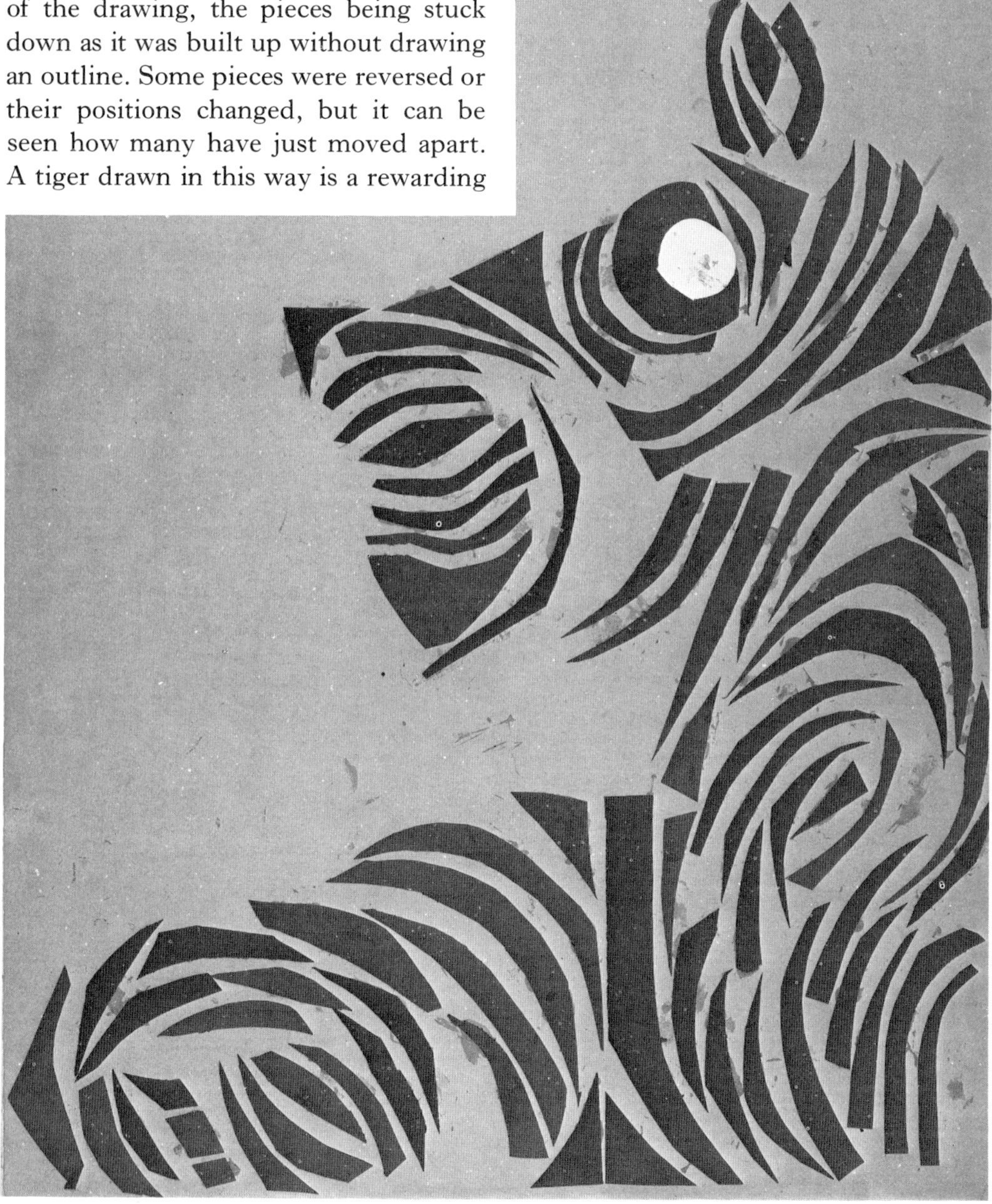

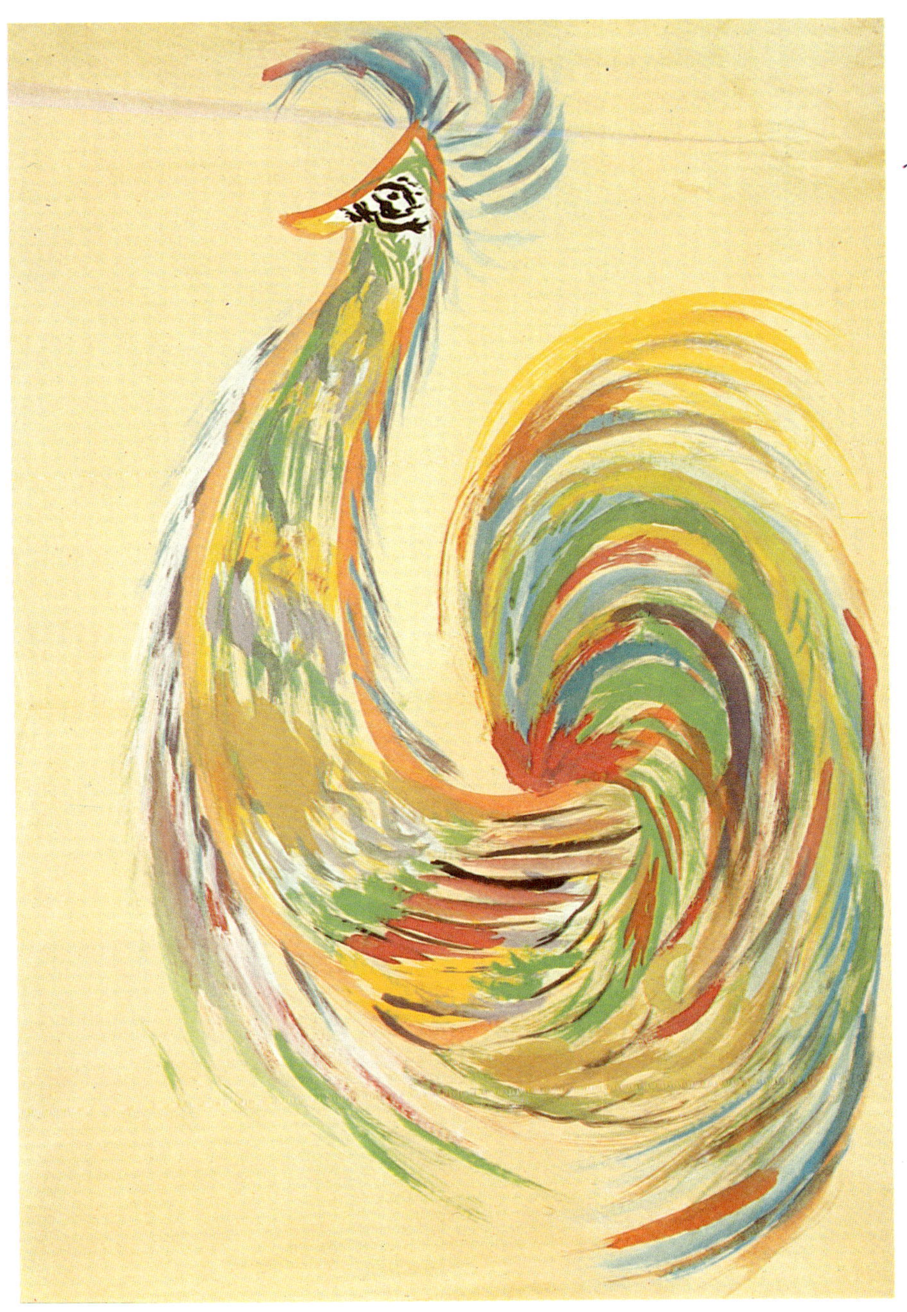

A bird of paradise—built up again without outline—from swirling strokes of large bristle brushes. The original was 27 in. high.

This drawing is a great contrast to the last. The proud strutting lines of the bird of paradise give way to the cold stillness of a misty day. What a contrast also to the winter scene on page 24. There is the same use of vertical and horizontal lines to give the effect of calm, the trees motionless in the freezing air, but the means by which the mood is achieved are quite different.

The marks of this drawing were printed. The unusual 'drawing instrument' used can be seen—real leaves. The leaves have been translated into trees—study of a leaf will reveal a reflection in its stem and veins of the growth pattern of a tree. The trees have been printed one by one and built up into a composition. This has the same meaning in drawing as when words are put together in a carefully arranged manner to tell a story.

To make a drawing like this a small roller is needed—cheap to buy or easy to make. Ink or paint is rolled on to the leaves and these are pressed on to the paper with a covering sheet. If two rollers are available one is used to ink the leaf and the ink is transferred to the other by rolling it over the inked leaf. The transferred image is then rolled on to the paper. The ground in this drawing was rolled on directly. The winter sun, huge and red, was printed with a potato. A potato is a splendid mark maker and may be used with great skill. It is not a childish thing to use at all.



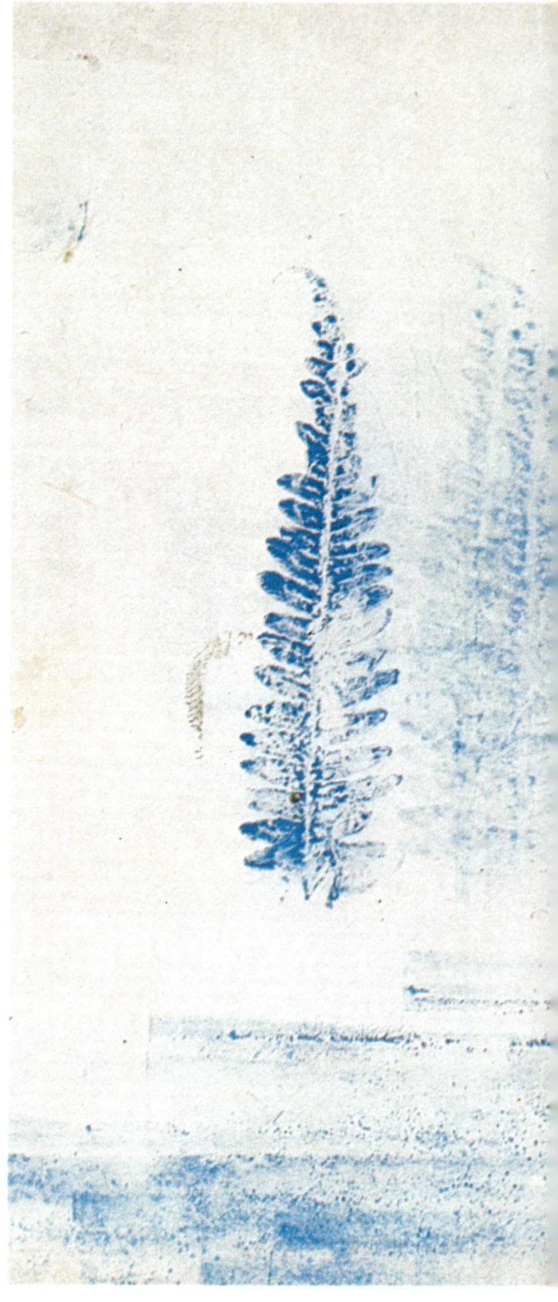

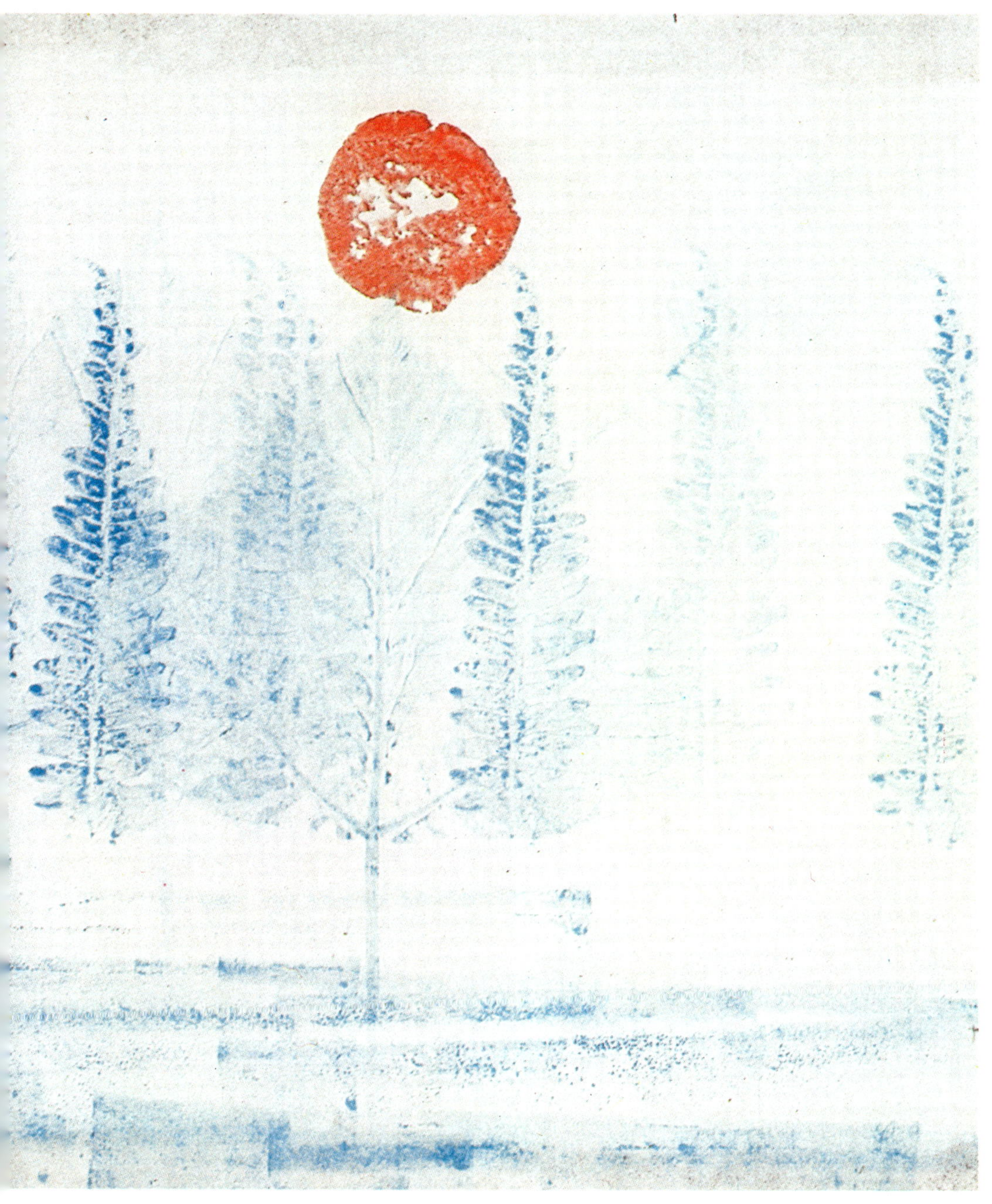

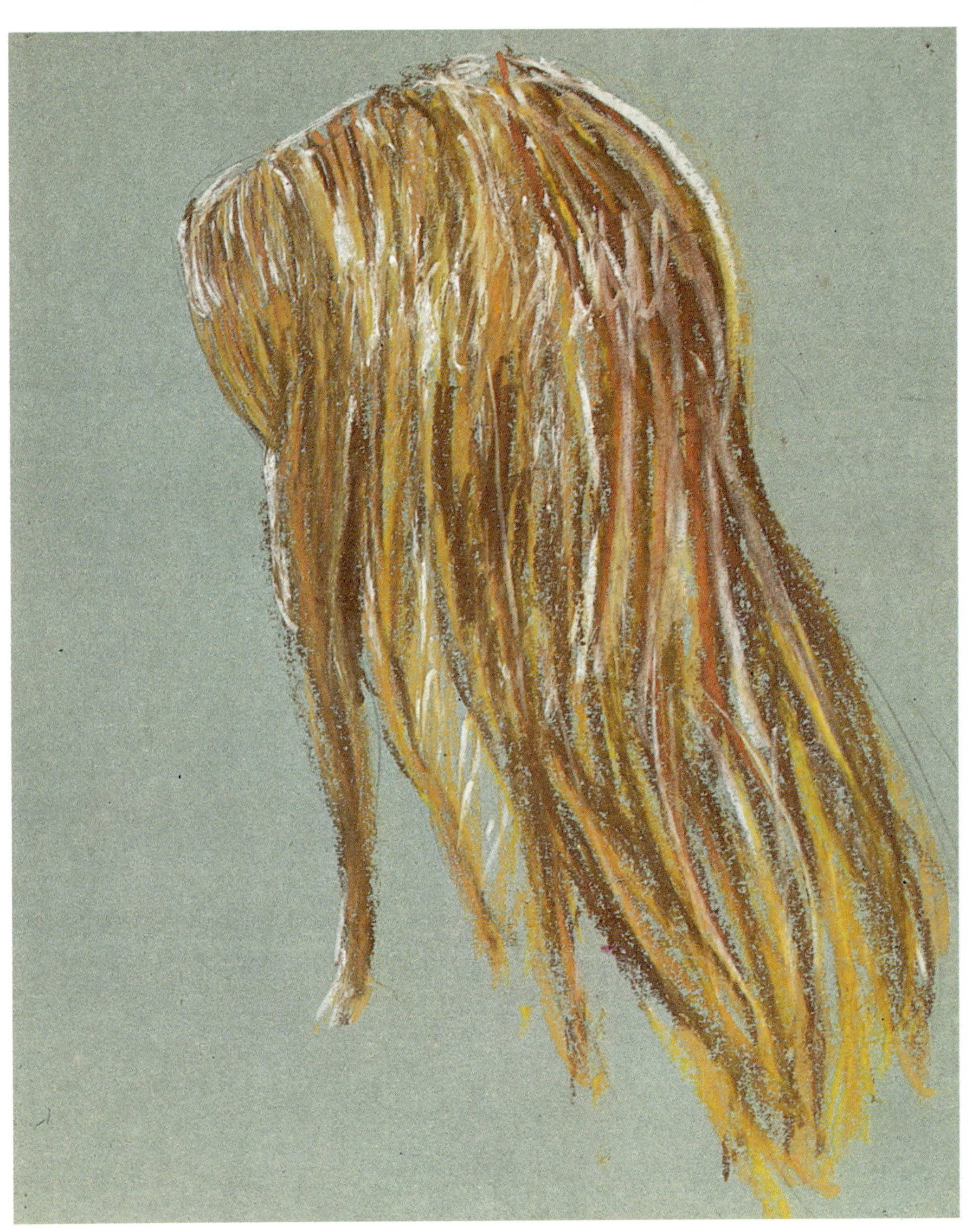

The texture of hair drawn with oil pastel.

# Drawing is using texture

When you stroke a pet cat or guinea pig you feel the soft silkiness of its fur. Fur has texture. We learn about most textures through the sense of touch. Stone, sand, velvet, a tortoise, corrugated cardboard, a sea urchin, cast iron, a pebble beach, the moon, weathered wood and a buttercup-spangled meadow all have texture.

Some textures grow naturally like the bark of a tree; some, like the pitted burnt clay of a single brick and the built-up texture of a whole wall, are man-made; some are caused by wind and water wearing things away, the burrowing activities of insects, and just old age. Textures are produced because these actions bring about variations in the structure of things, and particularly in their surfaces. Textures come in all shapes and sizes and in all materials. Take a long look around you at this moment and you will see a considerable number. Don't forget yourself!

When we touch a texture and feel the quality of a surface we have a tactile experience. We learn about things by touching them when we are old as well as when we are young. It is a pity that 'Do not touch' notices are so common because touching is such a splendid way of learning about things and often essential. By stroking them, or holding them we feel whether they are bristly, harsh, pitted, silky or polished, hard, firm or soft. It is an interesting study to make a collection of textured things, and grade them according to their degree of roughness or richness of surface. This can be a very sophisticated exercise.

A degree of roughness is, of course, not a necessary quality of texture, although it most often is. Nor can all textures be experienced with our hands. Some are visual and not tactile. The printed words on this page make a visual texture, and many visual textures are built up in the process of drawing. Marble has considerable visual texture, but it is smooth. Its texture comes essentially from the veins and blotches which mark its surface. These are discerned by seeing, but not by touch. Many sea shells are like this, their glossy smoothness marked with brilliant patterns of spots or stripes.

Others have both kinds of texture: they are ridged, pitted or spiky and have surface patterns. The textures of some things have to be 'felt' without touch because they are very large or a considerable distance away. The moon is only available as a tactile experience to a very select group of astronauts, but we can see its texture through a pair of binoculars, and this is confirmed by the astronauts who have found it very rough in their moonbuggy. A tree possesses not only the rough texture of its bark, but the vast rich texture formed by its crown of countless leaves changing constantly in the wind.

Texture then is the variation in a surface. It can be tactile or 'real' in the sense that it can be felt. It can be visual or 'apparent' in that it can be seen. Some things with real texture can only be experienced by seeing, and by experience we learn to feel even real texture without touching. Everyone knows that a hedgehog is prickly. Everyone knows that velvet is deliciously soft. We know from observation and knowledge that diving headfirst through a holly hedge is likely to be a

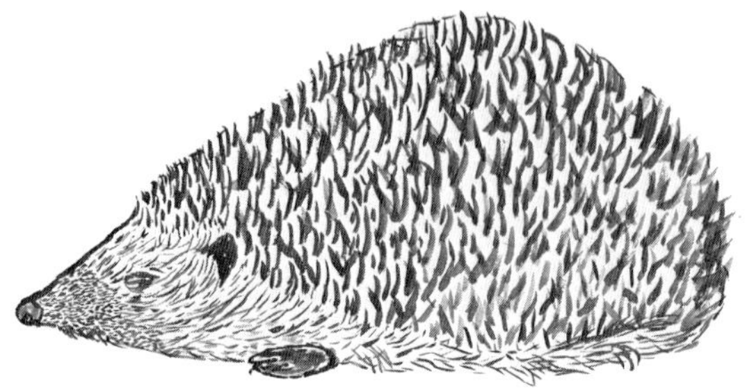

painful experience! However, things should be touched gently when it is proper to do so. Some things can be very surprising.

In drawing, texture is very important. Using texture it is possible to show much more clearly the difference between an orange and a tomato, a tennis ball and a golf ball, a steel breastplate and a sweater. Most of the drawings which we do involve the translation of textures into drawing marks which will give the character of those textures. Even when it is not the object of a drawing to report on the appearance of things, textures will very often be made up to give richness and variety to the drawing.

Once again, it is helpful in the task of

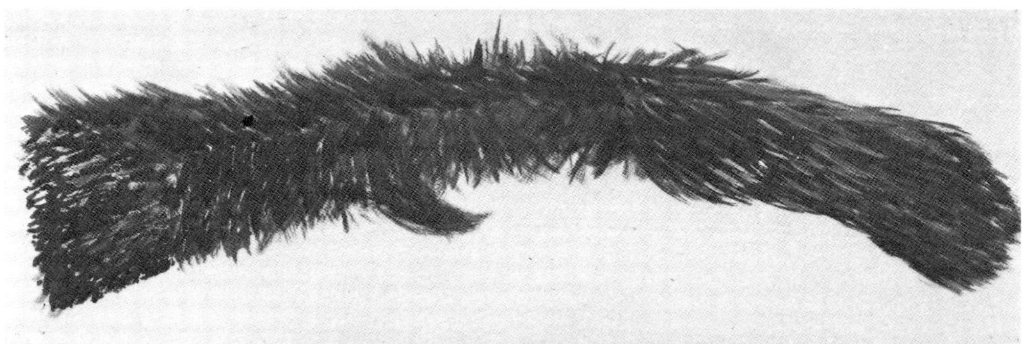

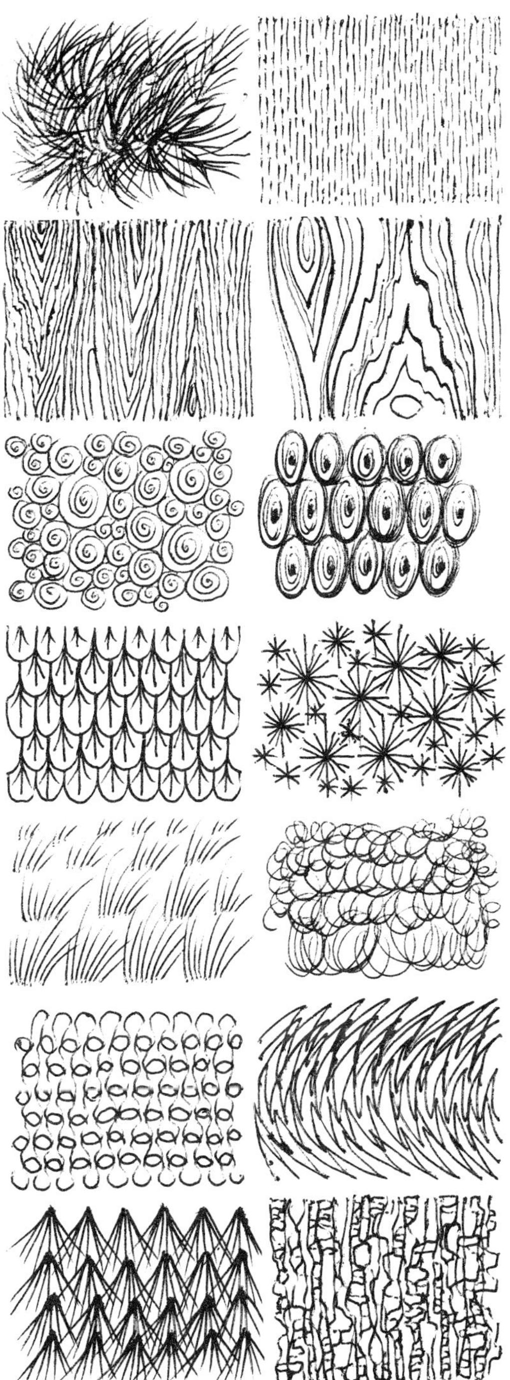

representing the surface quality of an object, whether small as a pebble or large as a range of mountains, to choose the drawing materials which are best for the purpose. It is necessary to remember that the choice of paper and the way the drawing tool is drawn across it will make their own contribution to the result. It should not be difficult to decide which choice will best represent fish scales, hair, crumbling stone, insect-bored wood, thistles, thick wool, or shiny steel. Unusual methods or materials produce interesting results—drawing on one piece of paper and blotting off on to another, drawing with ink on damp paper, spattering ink from an old toothbrush painted and drawn across the back of a knife, or using wax or gum resist. Rubbings may be made as part of the drawing process.

## Lines make texture

Opposite are some textures made up of lines drawn with a ballpoint pen. You should try to produce as many as you can with each drawing medium. Some will grow from reference to real things. Others will be made up from imagination. Build up some with tiny controlled finger movements, others with large sweeping strokes. A vast collection might be built up on squares of paper rather like a stamp collection, or each developing series might work up into an actual drawing—a well-farmed landscape, a rock-strewn desert with cacti and dead trees, a grand lady clad in fine clothes and jewels, or complicated abstract patterns can be built up. But whatever approach is used, it is the variety of textures which can be produced which matters. This is mark-making with endless possibilities.

## Dots make texture

It will be remembered that lines begin life as dots. The importance of dots, splotches, minute circles, and similar marks in the making of textures will not need stressing if you look at a piece of cork, a sponge, a pebble, a broken brick, or a saucer of bubbles made with liquid detergent. Look at them for enhanced quality of texture under a magnifying glass, and it will be seen even more clearly how a surface is pitted with holes, or built up with mounds or ridges, or glistening spheres. There are fantastic new worlds to be observed through a magnifying glass, and a microscope will reveal even more—and more the greater its power. Both these instruments should be obtained if possible. They more than repay their cost.

The broken surfaces of all these wonderful little worlds which can be held in the hand are often best textured not with lines, but with dots. Small dots, large dots, blotchy dots, dots which crawl and creep into one another, dots which stand aloof, dots which splash on to the paper, hollow dots—hundreds and hundreds of them, building up into fantastic textures. How many different kinds of dots there are only experiment will reveal. Try making them with pens of all kinds, crayon, pastel, paint—a pencil is rather weak for producing dots. As with lines, it is good exercise to make up patterns, but all of them can be based on what can be seen around you if ideas run out. The things which can be seen are in any case our principal concern in drawing.

With large subjects like landscapes, a big drawing instrument will be necessary if dot technique is used or the drawing will take a very long time. Normally, dots are combined with short strokes and lines, and the results can make a considerable impression. The pen drawings of Van Gogh are brilliant examples of such a technique. It should not be difficult to think of a suitable landscape subject. A cornfield and a beach with crumbling cliffs are obvious examples. One of the advantages of the dot technique is that, if you are still rather nervous about your drawing — quite unnecessarily — 'mistakes' are so easy to lose. They just become part of the texture. Opposite there are panels of spontaneous experiments with a pen, and over the page, textures made with the objects drawn being looked at.

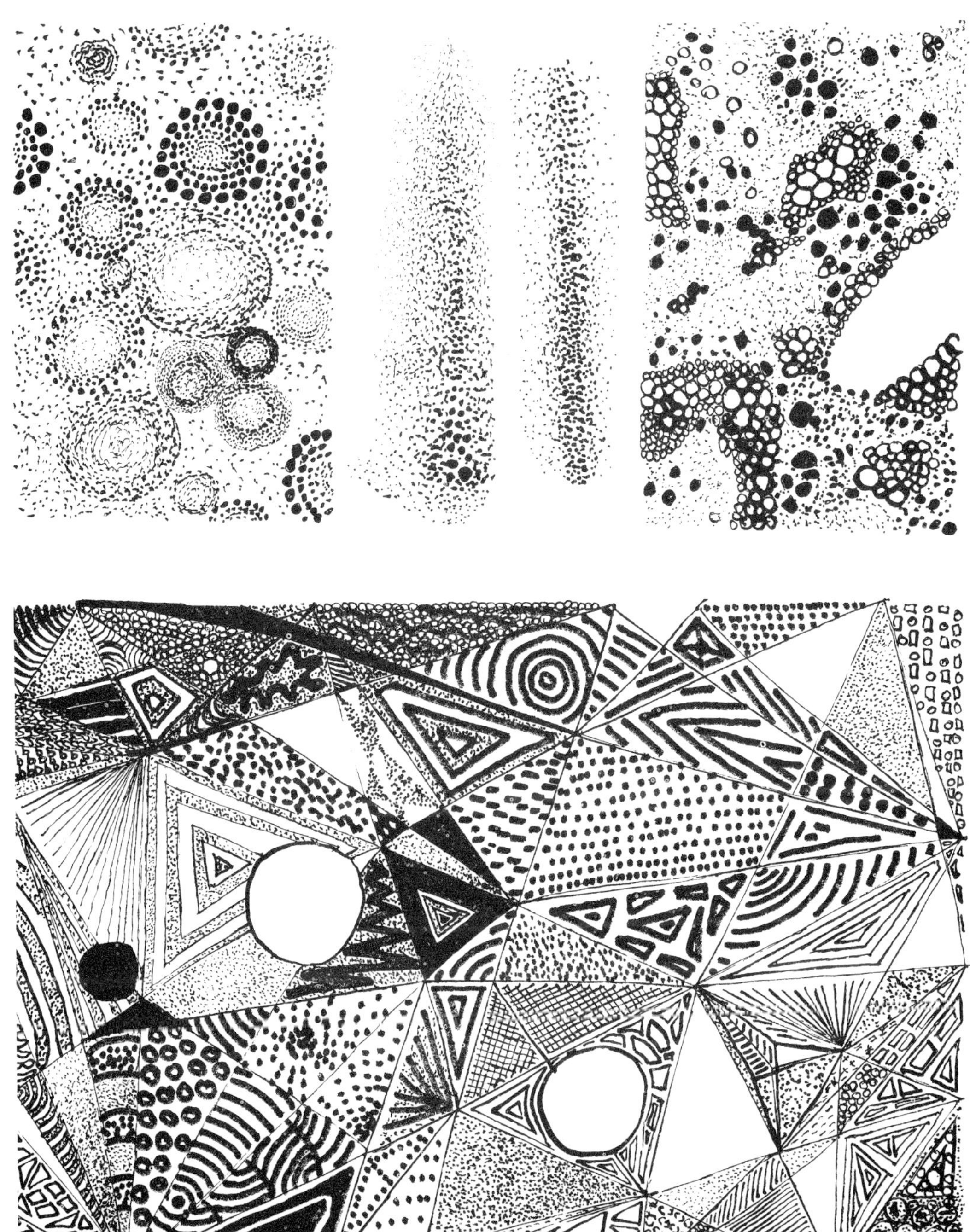

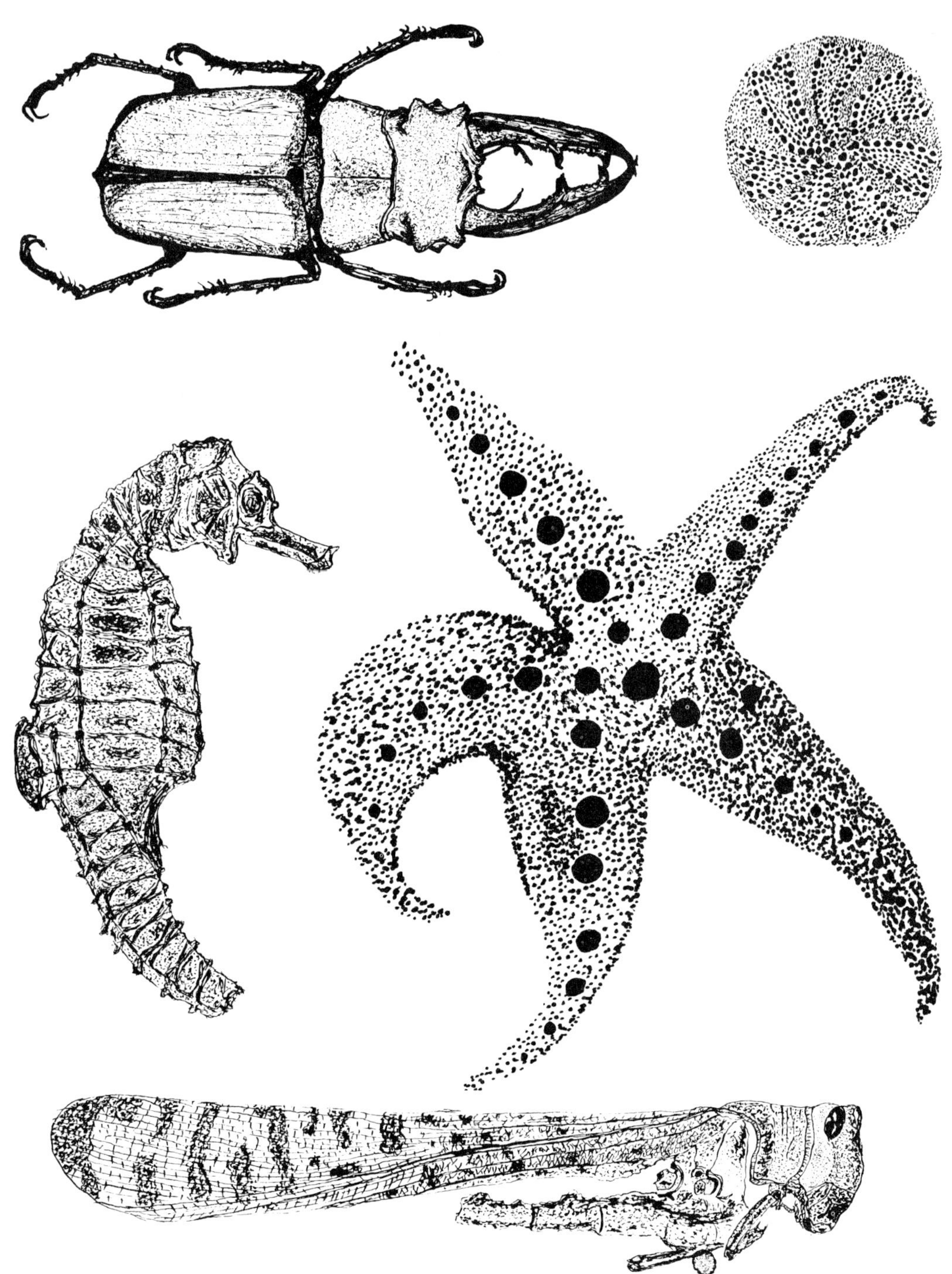

Some of the work is very delicate and most of these dot drawings were little larger than these reproductions. To develop to the highest level your natural capacity to draw, you need to practise in this way so that you are able to use fine finger movements when it is necessary, or great sweeping hand—even arm—strokes when they are called for. Delicacy does not involve lack of decision or strength. Leonardo da Vinci was so strong that he could straighten horse-shoes, but his drawings are exquisitely delicate.

You will be able to think of many other ways in which dots can be put together to make intriguing textures. Try some which convey information other than about surfaces—fireworks exploding, water spraying from a fountain. Using a dot for each, it is possible to show crowds of people, or city-square pigeons burst-ing in alarm into the sky and whirling about. Their movement is shown with a pattern of dots. With the development of skill and confidence, be more am-bitious and make each dot a complete drawing! This was done with lines of rest in the winter landscapes on pages 24 and 30–31 —they became trees and ground. It just takes longer because each 'mark' must become a more complex series of marks rather as if it had come under a magnifier.

More 'accidental' ways of producing texture include spattering, dabbing, dragging, blotting and printing with appropriate material—the old tooth-

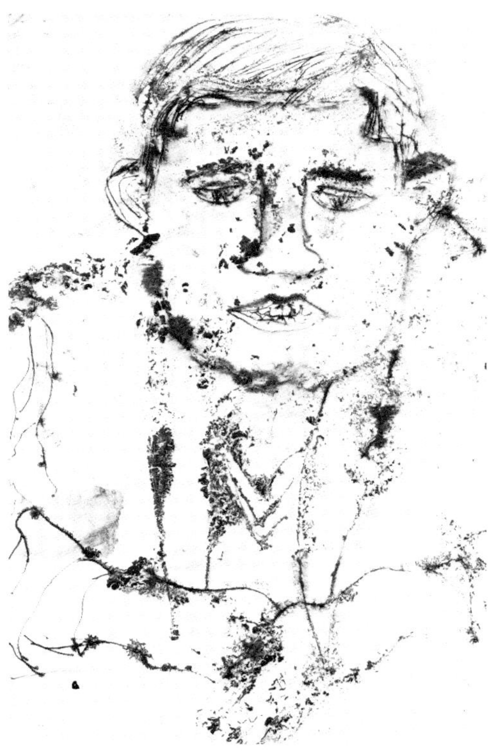

brush already mentioned, sponges, pieces of plastic foam, coarse paper, screwed-up paper, sacking. The drawing above was made on wet paper with waterproof ink. Often greater control is possible if the ink or paint, charcoal or graphite powder is applied to the tool indirectly with a pad or brush rather than dipping it straight into the pot. A toothbrush can hold a lot of ink and it is surprising how far it can travel! The shape of the draw-ing may be masked with pieces of paper or a shaped cut-out mask, or a piece of textured paper can be made first and the image cut out for finishing after mount-ing on another piece of paper. Cut out images will be considered later.

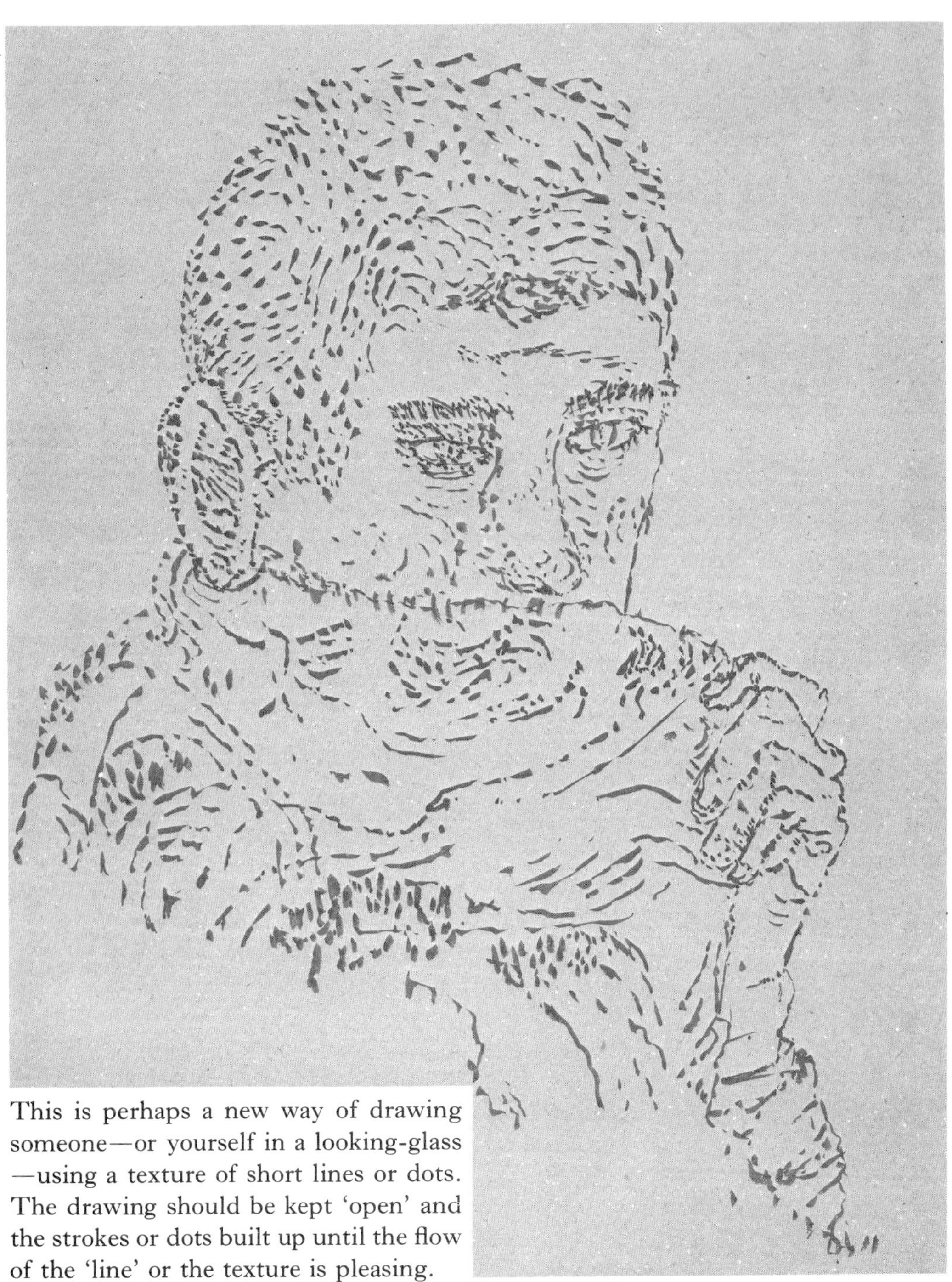

This is perhaps a new way of drawing
someone—or yourself in a looking-glass
—using a texture of short lines or dots.
The drawing should be kept 'open' and
the strokes or dots built up until the flow
of the 'line' or the texture is pleasing.

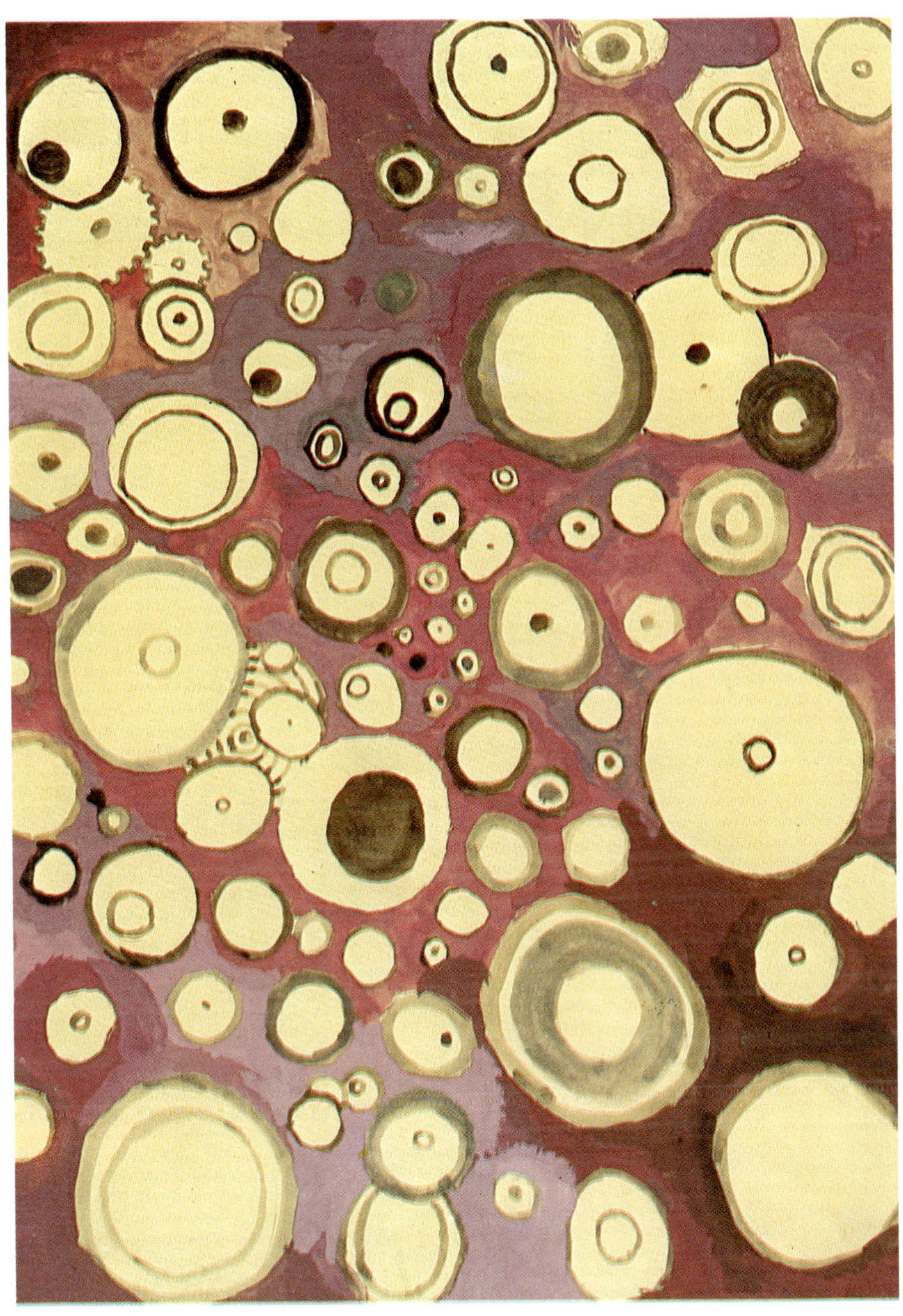

A pitted surface magnified and changed
into a pattern of circles and spots.

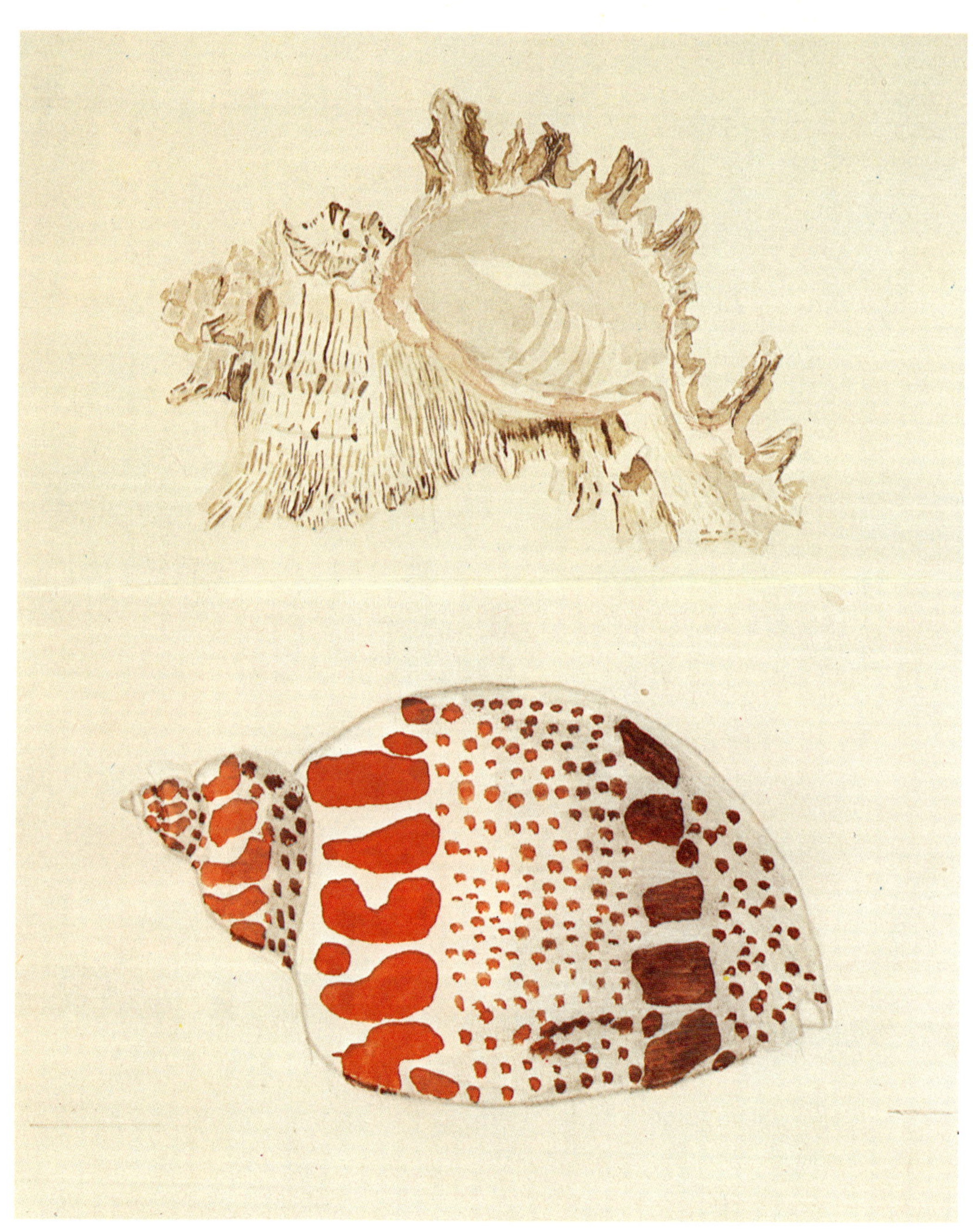

A rough shell and a smooth shell, but both textured.

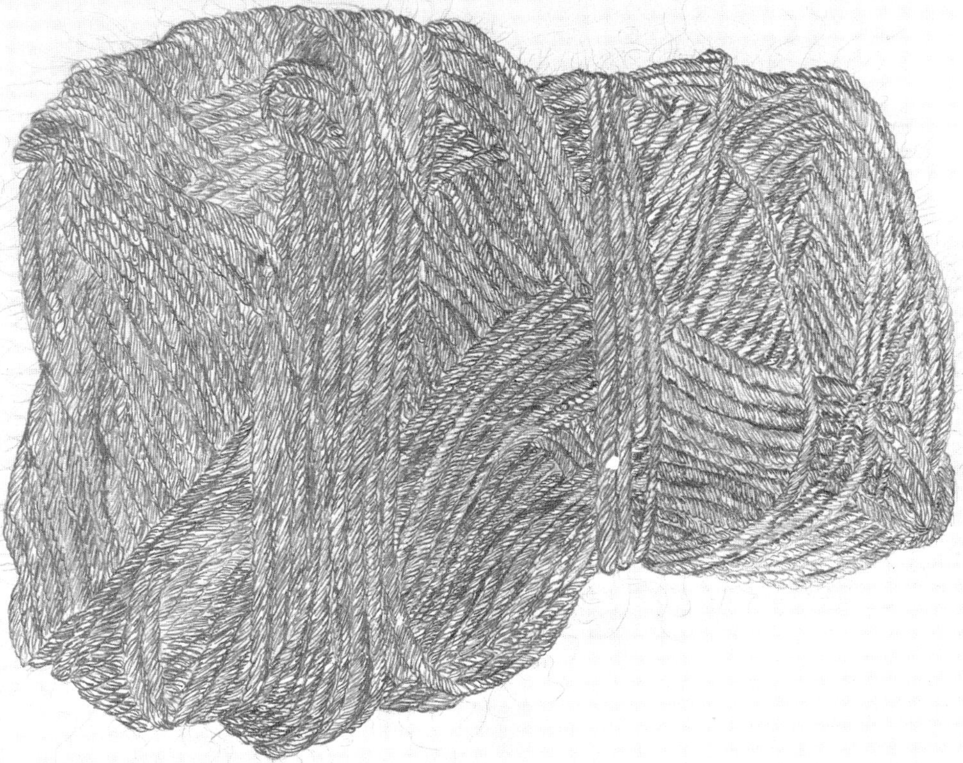

The hank of string was drawn with a pencil and the original is 14 in. long. It was made large so that the texture could be drawn strongly, and to keep the lines open. Notice the whiskers round the edges. A good artist sees everything although he may choose to omit things.

Below are rubbings of the texture of the two sides of a piece of frosted glass. Surprising discoveries like this may often be made by the process of rubbing.

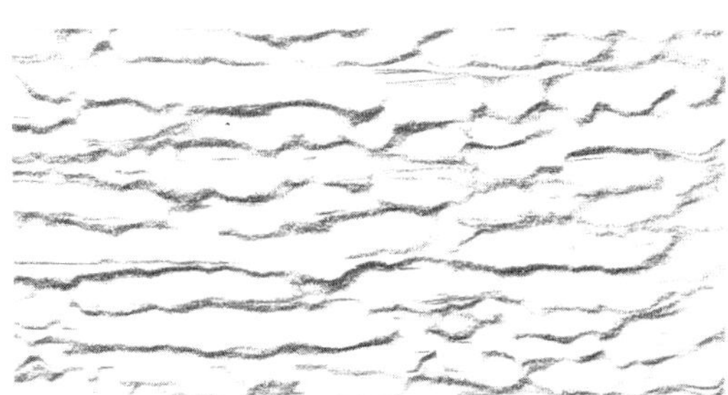

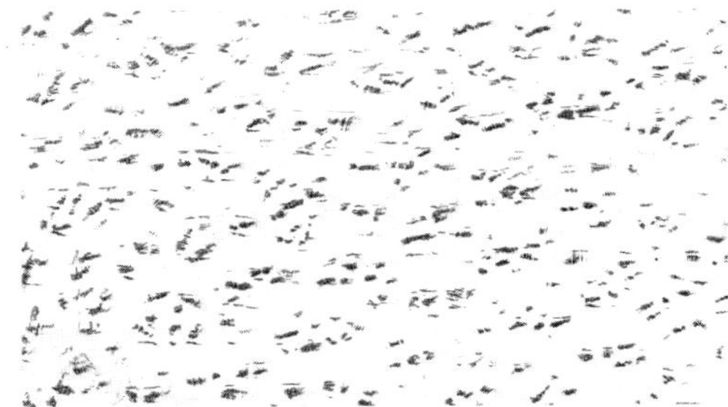

Here are some contrasts in the use of texture. The head and body of the first bird were made from rubbings cut out and stuck to a black surface textured with lively blobs of white paint.

The hawk was drawn in pen and ink and shows how richly the texture of feathers can be built up, and the variety and rhythm which can be achieved. The fine buzzard is in pencil, and shows the vigour with which this much misused instrument can be used.

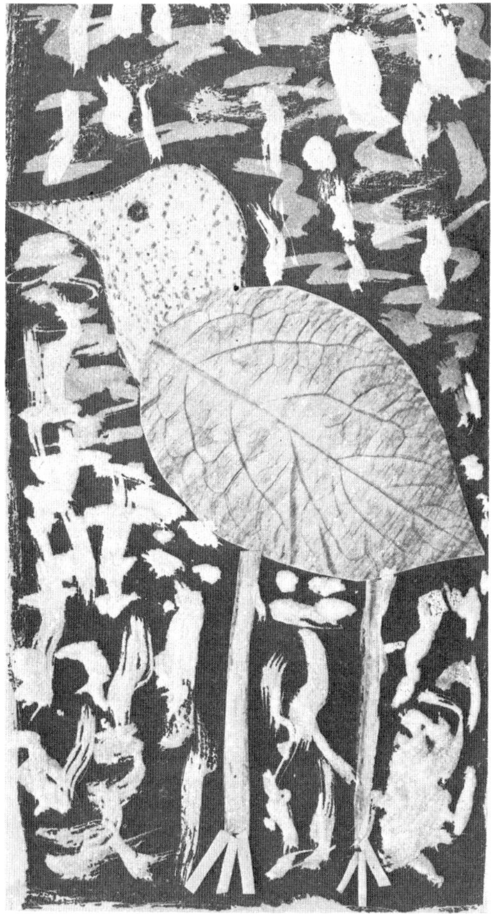

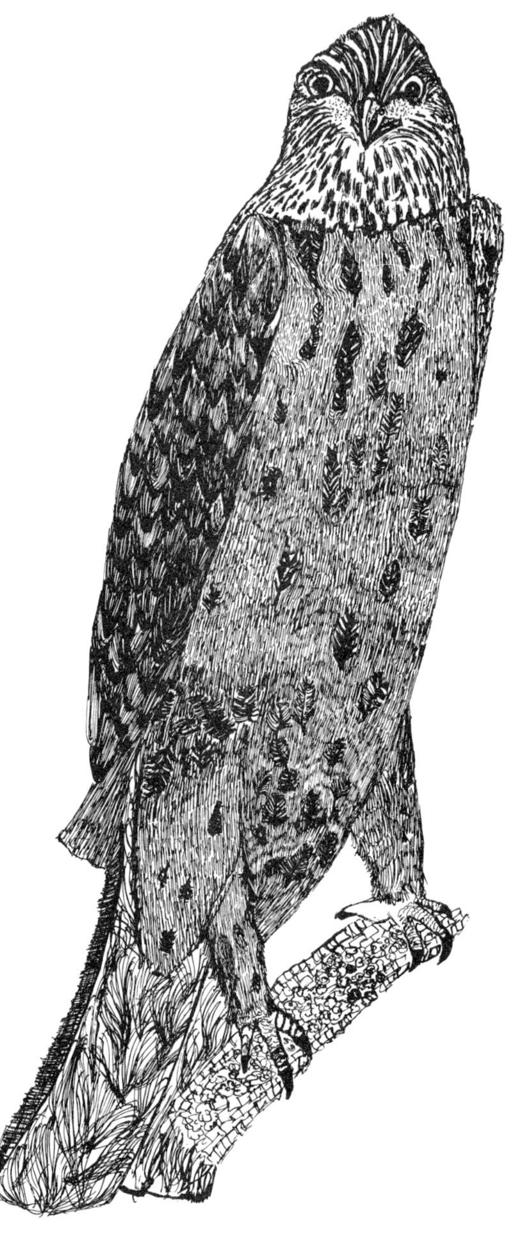

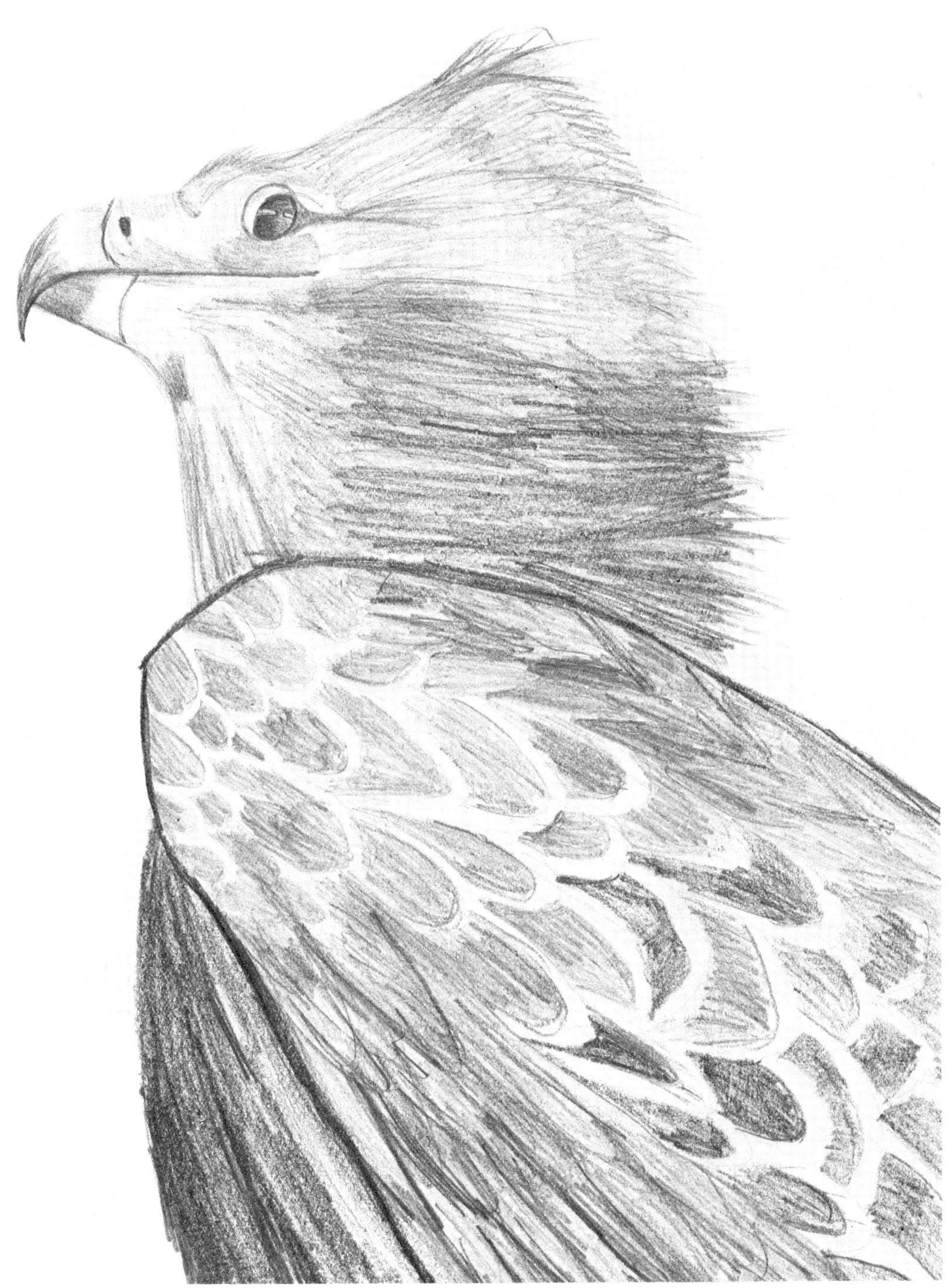

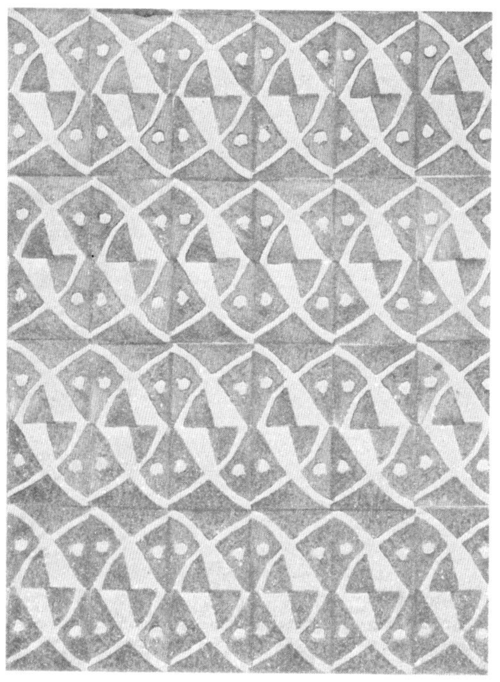

## Texture and pattern

The word pattern has occurred several times already, and many of the drawings reproduced are fine patterns. It will have become clear that the word means more than the repeated design on wallpaper or a dress. Man is often referred to as a pattern maker, and it is rewarding to think about what this really means.

In a drawing a pattern exists when the parts work together as a unit. This may be done in a regular way as in a brick wall where the parts are all the same shape and size. The potato print on the left is such a pattern. Or it may be done in an irregular way as in a stone wall, where the stones are all more or less rectangular in shape, but not of the same dimensions. The pamphlet cover of 'some of our class' on the left is such a pattern. Some similarity of shape, size or rhythm, tone, colour or texture is necessary to give the essential unity of a pattern. This is why too much variety in a drawing—or any work of art, including architecture—is disturbing. It upsets unity, appears confused, and makes the observer feel restless. When there is real satisfaction with something we have done, it is usually because in some way the harmony of unity has been achieved. A heap of bricks dumped from a truck and seen from a distance would not have an easily-discernible pattern—although if it were looked at hard and long enough some sort of pattern would almost certainly be found—but it would have obvious texture.

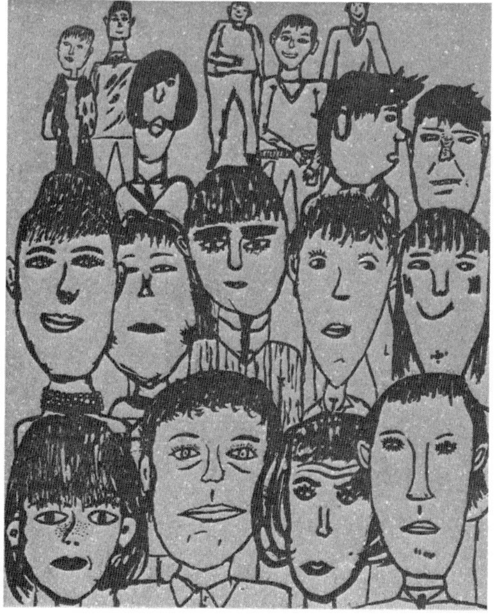

Patterns might be called textures which have been put together in a more orderly way: some of the pen textures on page 35 are obvious patterns. Patterns almost always emerge when even the most tangled texture is seen close up. On the right is a drawing of a soft feather from a feather duster. It has texture. Under the drawing is a magnified photogram of a small part of such a feather. It has a quite regular pattern. Allowances must be made for a degree of irregularity, because nothing in nature is ever absolutely regular or absolutely the same. That is one of the reasons why the natural world is always so interesting, and so rich a source of inspiration for drawing. Sometimes tactile texture and visual pattern are almost the same, as in the shell of a tortoise.

When a shape is repeated using a constant rhythm, it builds up into a regular repeat pattern. This is part of drawing. Using drawing marks notebook covers can be designed or, with the easy dyes which are now available, you can transform a plain T-shirt with a pattern. These can be done with any suitably-sized drawing medium using rhythmic writing movements. Repetition is easier and quicker if drawing marks are cut into a block and printed. Care and precision in adding print to print are important, and if this is done with a well-produced block, patterns of fine craftsmanship are possible.

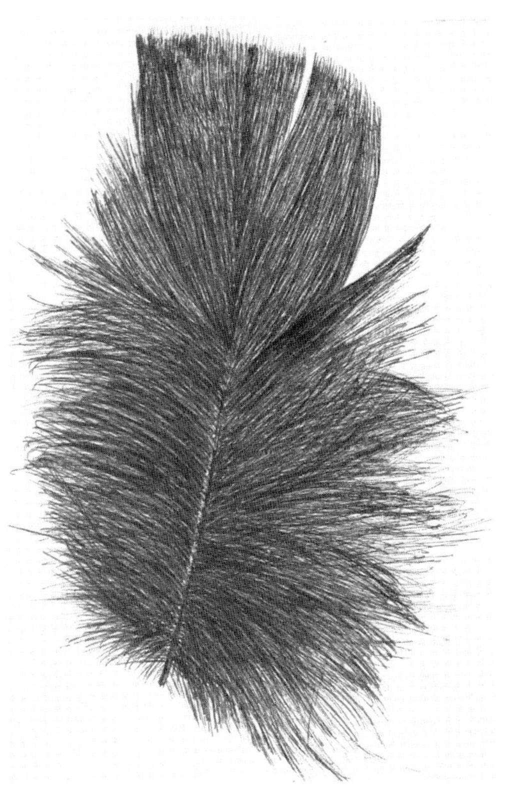

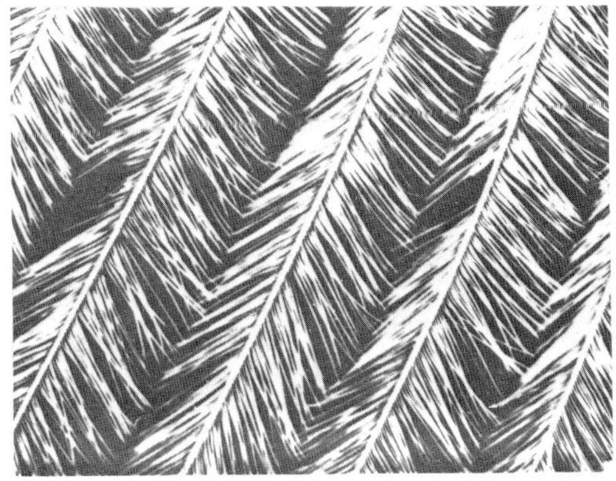

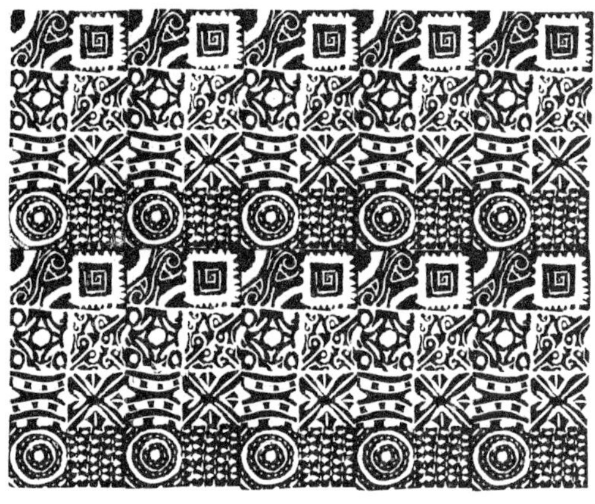

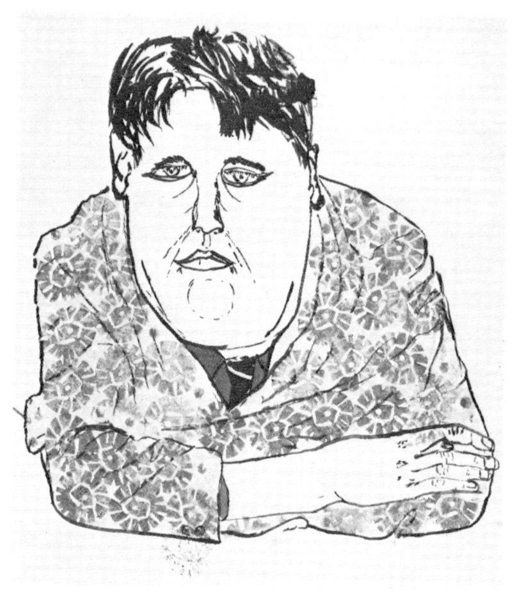

This design began as practice in making marks and texture with a lino cutter before producing pictorial work like the owls in this book. It ended as pattern, because the textured block was repeated in printing. Can you see the block unit? Below is a notebook case covered with a pattern drawn with a fine brush in writing rhythm. Can you see the rhythm? Line drawings can be developed in many ways with printed marks. Here simple potato-cut blocks have added both pattern and colour—the latter unseen on this page. Try making a simple block— always the most effective—with one or two cut marks in a carefully smoothed potato block and see how many different regular patterns can be produced from it.

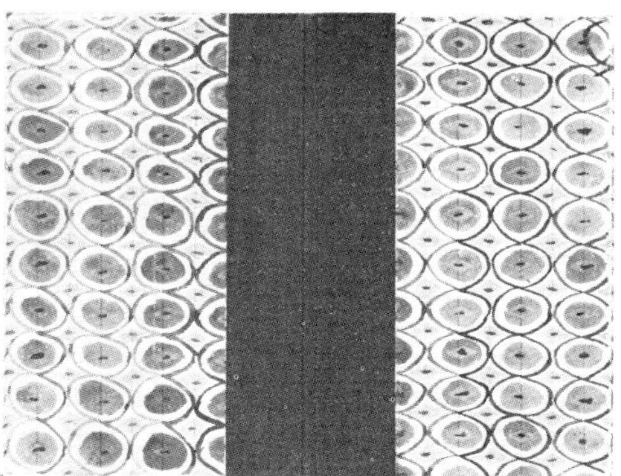

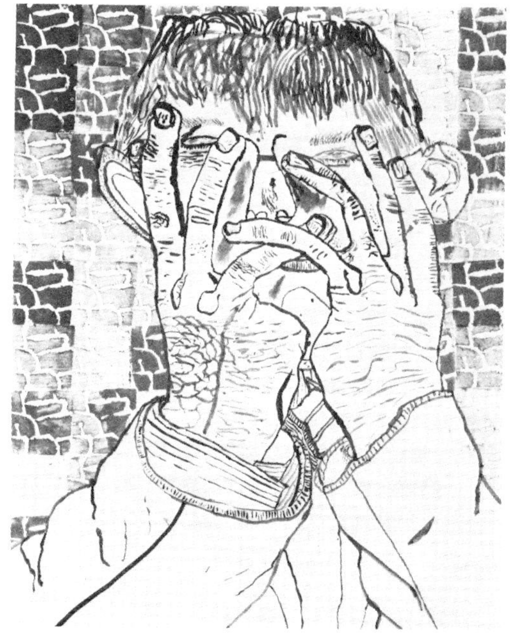

# Drawing is making shapes

Everything has shape. Even a line is a long, narrow shape. As young children our first drawings were scribbles; by doing these we learnt to control the movements of our hands. We drew lines, and then began to use them to enclose parts of the surface of the paper. We drew enclosed shapes. When an enclosed shape is made, a shape is also made outside it. In drawing it is particularly necessary to observe that not only do objects have shape, but also the spaces between them and around them. Seeing these spaces and the relationship of which they are a part is as important as seeing the solid shape of things. They make most interesting patterns and can be drawn as themselves. On the next page is a drawing of a plant and below it is a picture which looks like two monsters standing by a tree—it is really made of some of the space shapes in the plant drawing. A few moments' observation will reveal which ones. The drawing of the cat pacing through the flowers is an interesting combination of solid and space shapes. Look at the side of the cat. When spaces are seen as well and as naturally as solids, a most exciting 'new' way of looking at things will have been developed and drawing improves enormously, with a much greater unity particularly apparent.

The line which encloses a shape is an outline—a line which shows where the outer edge of something is. Most of the drawings in this book were built up into shapes. They grew from the inside. They did not begin as enclosed shapes. Turn back to the two shell drawings on page 42. The top shell grew, mark being added to mark without an initial outline, while the bottom shell began as an outline, or enclosed, shape. The other marks were added because the artist wanted to say more about it. Most often he needs to. Outline drawings of a box seen end on, or a rectangular wire frame are not very satisfactory because it is difficult to tell which is which. More information is required. The making of drawings from the inside by a growing process usually inspires the giving of more information and that is why it has been dealt with first.

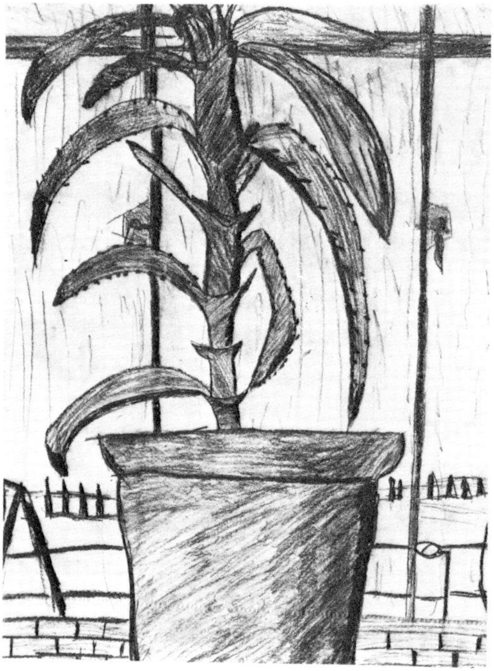

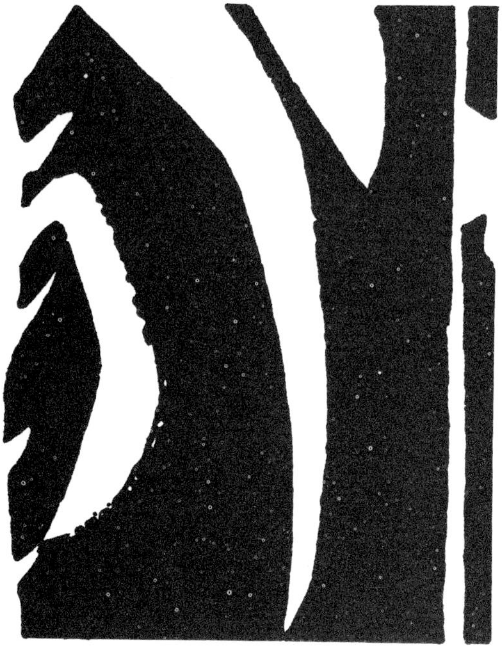

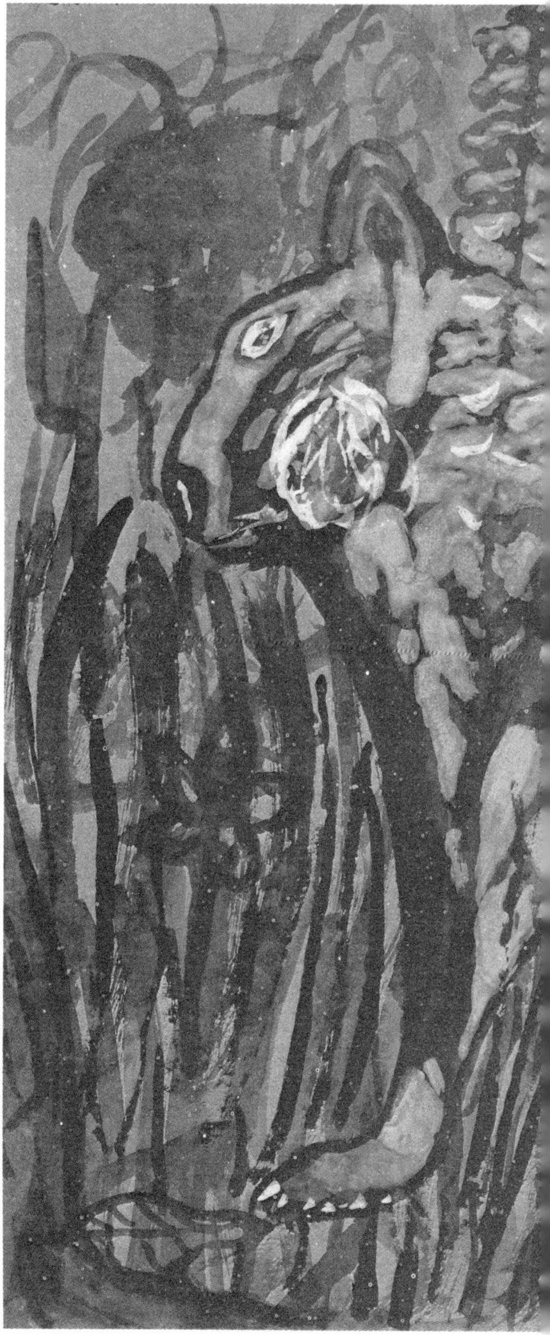

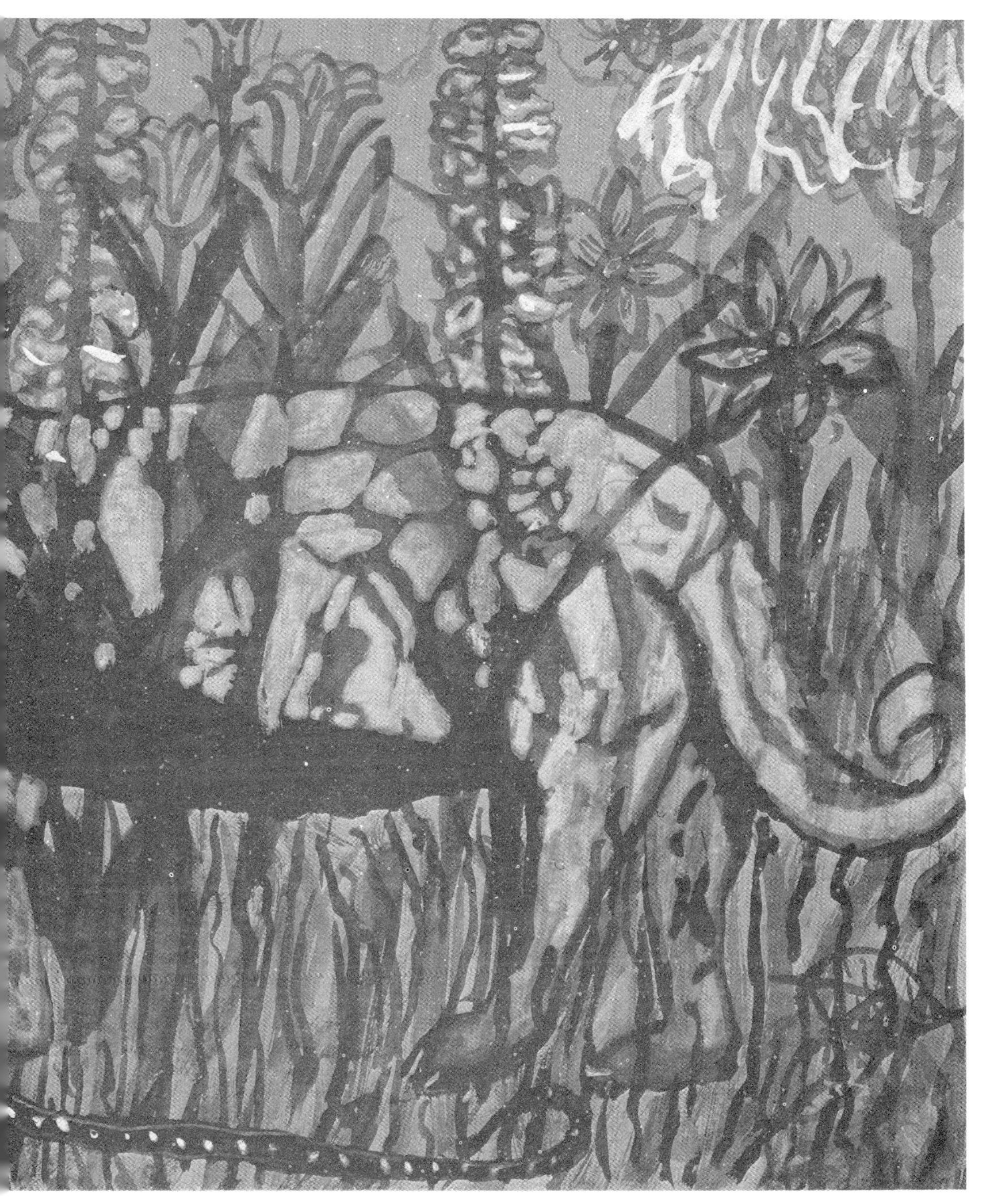

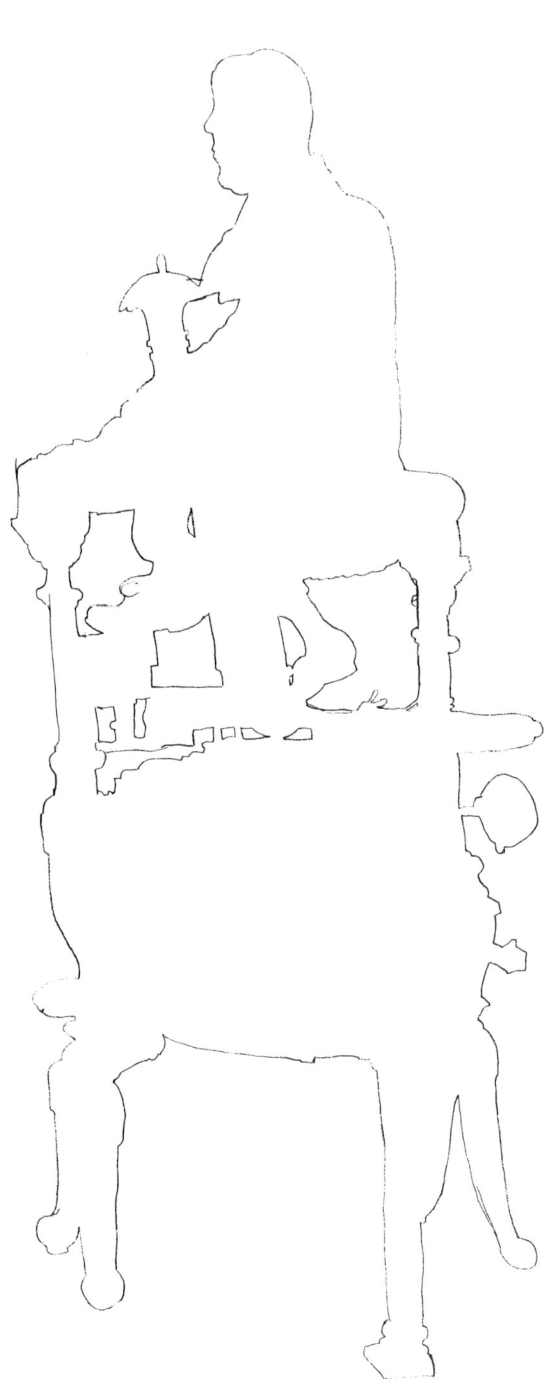

An interesting point is that almost all the drawings which people make naturally from the time when they are very young are outline drawings, and if it is a more complicated shape than an orange, by adding one outline to another; and yet this way of drawing seems to become more difficult as we grow older. There seem to be two reasons. First, too much of the shape has to be absorbed at once, and the more complicated the shape, the more difficult this is, and also we demand much more of our drawings without having had the necessary practice. The other reason is that too often shapes are taken for granted and we stop really seeing things. We carry fixed ideas in our minds labelled 'house shape', 'egg shape' and so on and draw those, and are dissatisfied with them. But, of course, there are hundreds of house shapes, all different, and quite a lot of egg shapes, although they do have something in common. A look at just three eggs will show how different they can be. Subtle differences must be observed by looking hard.

The drawing on the left is of the edges of a complicated shape—a boy sitting on the top of a printing press—and it required a lot of concentration. Labels do not help in making a drawing like this. An alert searching eye does. The advantage of making outline drawings is not only that they are marvellous practice.

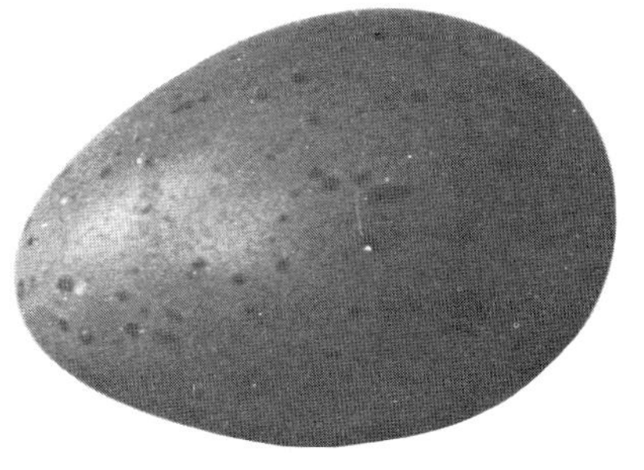

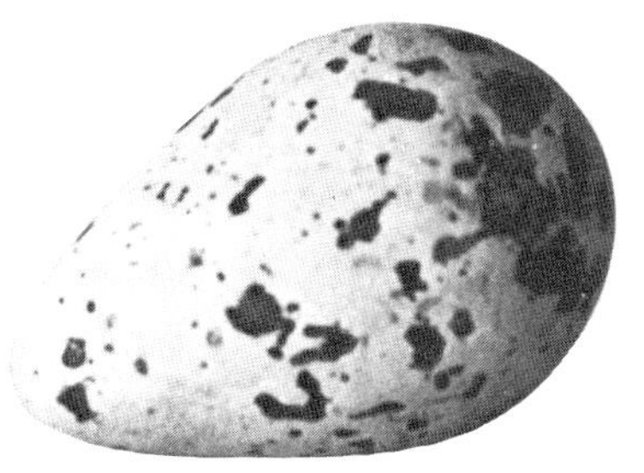

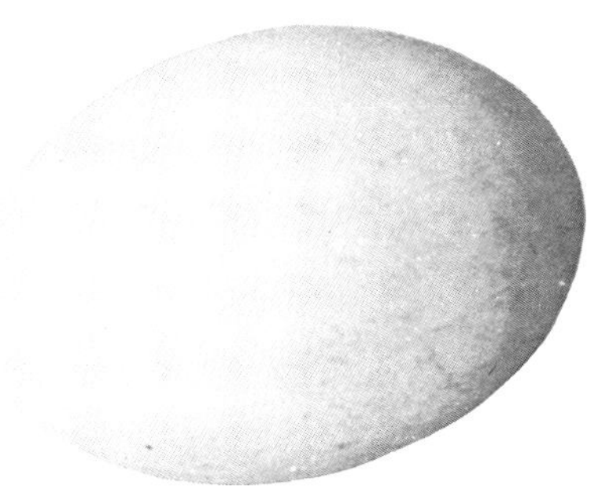

quired. For all drawing, we have to learn to see small differences between shapes —as with the eggs—and be able to measure them by eye as the drawing proceeds. Measuring to quite an accurate degree is possible by eye alone. But consider differences first. Draw typical shapes of different things which yet have something in common. Which view says most about a broom, this:

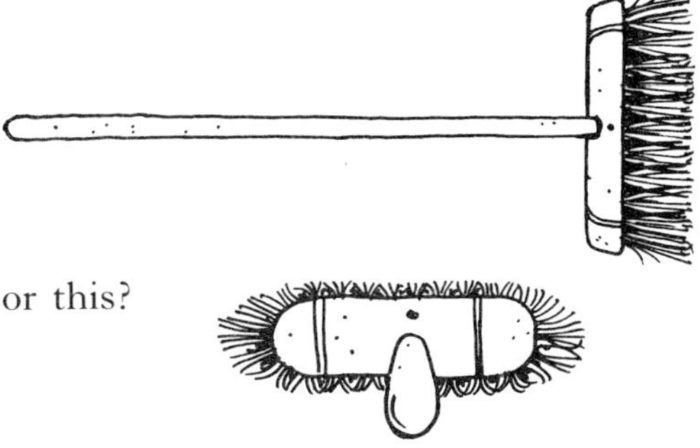

or this?

Try drawing clearly and carefully the typical views of a group of roughly similar shapes—broom, hammer, hoe, golf putter, paste spreader. Try a difficult group—tomato, orange, grapefruit, peach, apple. Look at the same stone from different viewpoints. See how subtly the views vary and yet relate to one another. Cut up a potato and see how the slices belong to a 'family'. In studying differences of this kind, it is often very helpful to isolate the shape and relate it to another simpler shape by looking at it through a rectangular hole cut in a piece of card, or using an empty 35mm transparency frame. One eye must be closed for this to be done effectively. Then it is easy to see space shapes and solid shapes, judge angles and lengths,

On many occasions they give enough information for a particular purpose, and they are usually more quickly done than growing-from-the-inside drawings. What has to be learnt is the process by which they can be made more accurate —to make them 'look right'. Then they are satisfying as records of things seen. Then they give the information re-

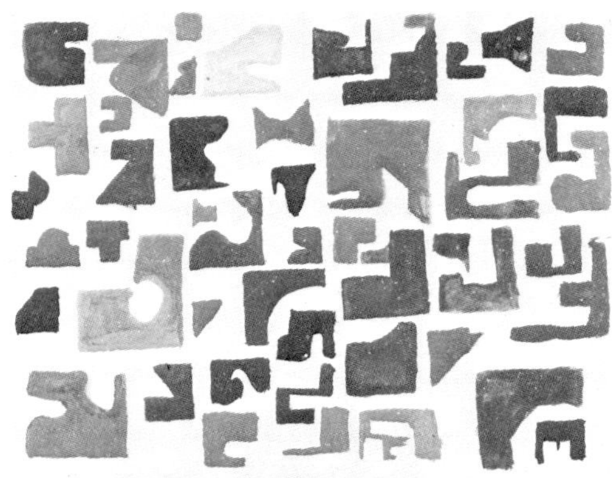

see that bits stick out halfway, or a third
of the way along, and so on. Practise
creating shape variations by taking a
shape and making a set of differences, as
in the painted squares above. Of course,
any reasonably simple shape may be
used, and the idea is to make each different from all the others, but retain a
family resemblance in spite of their
differences. In the original of the squares,
which is in colour, there is another family
relationship maintained by using various
shades of green, yellow green and green
blue. To change gradually from one
shape, for example a square, to another,
perhaps a circle, through a number of
stages each taking the change a little
further is interesting. Use cut-paper
shapes, 'drawing' the edges with scissors.

Another sort of relationship is created
when lines flow, either actually or in-
visibly, from one shape to another. This
is important in picture composition.

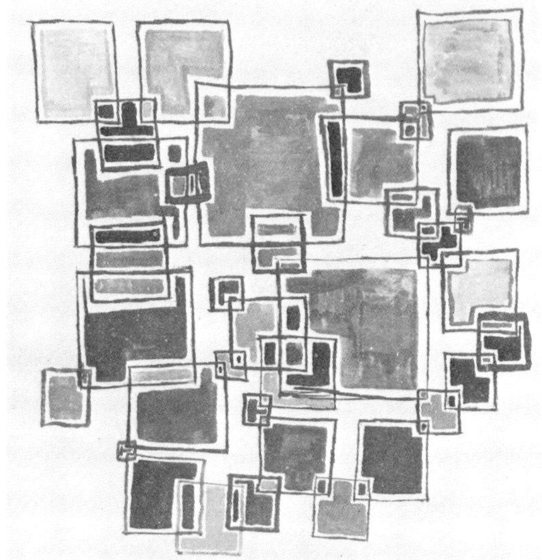

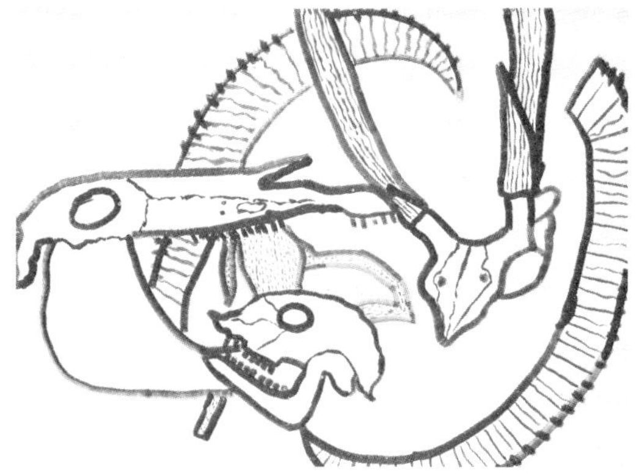

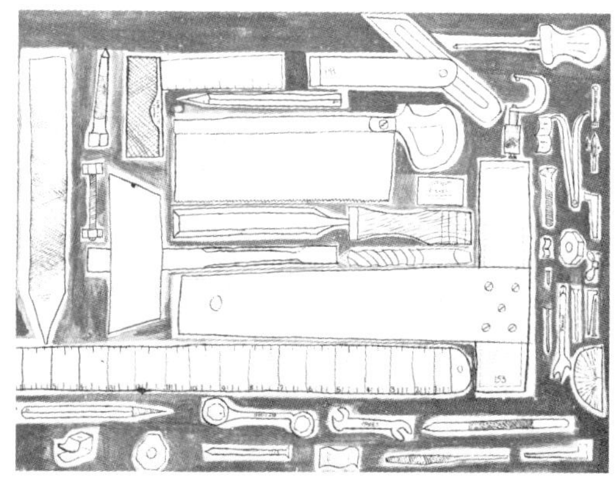

54

You will see this in the drawings of the squares, bones and tools. Notice how unified they seem, a unity brought about by this continuity of lines as well as the repetition of similar shapes. Notice also how in relationship they make new shapes. Overlapping shapes do this. Make your own designs of related shapes. Here are some other different, but related, shapes.

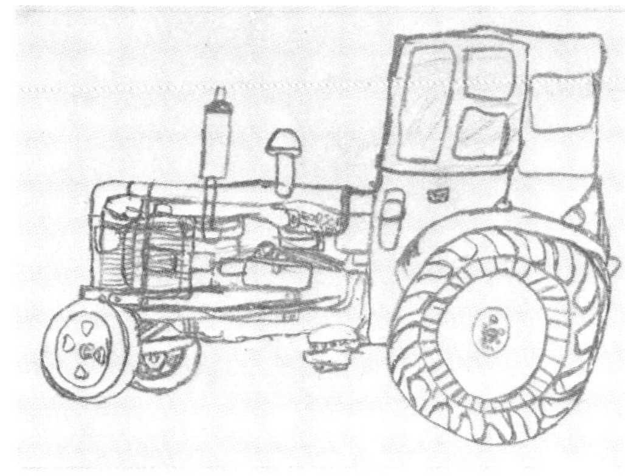

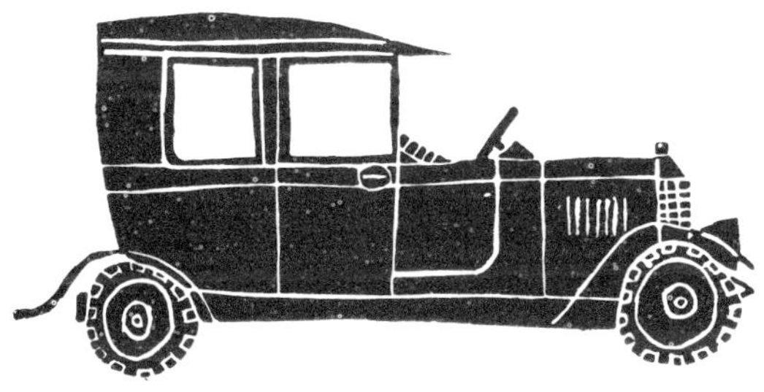

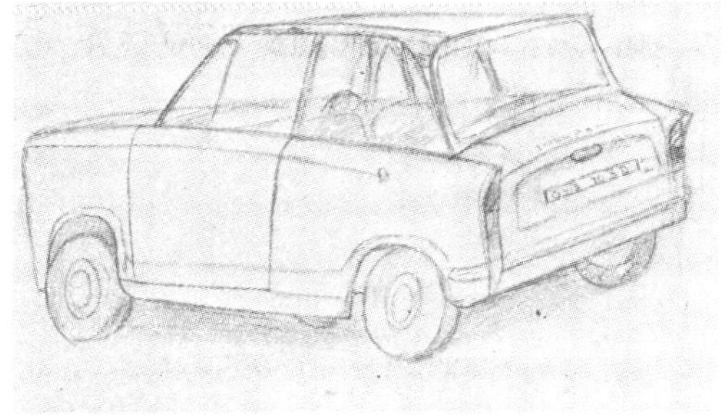

## Visual mathematics

Now—measuring by eye. To do this we stop glancing casually at things and put the whole power of the mind behind the eyes, using them in a kind of visual mathematics. Ideally this should be done from as early an age as possible, certainly as soon as the feeling begins that a drawing 'doesn't look right'.

If it is continued more and more as a person grows older, the more 'right' the drawings produced will become. How much measuring has to be done will depend on the subject, and how great the intention is to represent its shape accurately. It will be understood that measuring a complicated subject like a cathedral or a combine harvester might take quite a long time. Quite often a person will be happy with an impression, and that is very proper. Or it may be desired to exaggerate the character of something for emphasis, and that is very proper also. Accuracy in reporting the exact physical appearance of things is only one of the artistic tasks, and as mentioned already, what is felt is often at least as important. But even so, it will still have been necessary to have measured roughly, so that what is to be emphasized is known. A long low drawing of a skyscraper will not look very effective. How do we measure with our eyes?

First of all, it is necessary to look very hard at the shape which is to be drawn and to start thinking of lengths and widths, heights and angles, all in relationship to each other.

A person's head is a certain length in relationship to the length of the body, or the total height. Arms are so many 'heads' long. A nose is a fraction of a head long. Let us look at a simple shape and analyse it—take it apart in our minds, and put it together again on paper. Here is the shape:

If a number of people were asked to draw it, they might say that it looked like this:

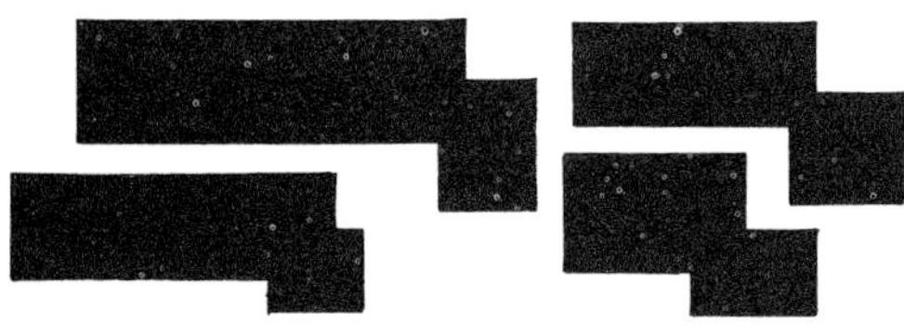

and as rough impressions these might satisfy. If a more accurate drawing is wanted, it might be analysed like this— checking each thought. 'The shape consists of a rectangle growing into what appears to be a square in the bottom right-hand corner, roughly so (1).' 'I will draw the long top line first' (2). 'The left-hand vertical of the long part of the shape seems to be half its length and at right-angles to it. I will draw this' (3). 'I will complete the rectangle' (4) and (5). 'The right-hand side of the square seems to be the same length as the short left-hand side of the rectangle. This means that the square is half the size of the rectangle. Now how does it fit on to the corner?' 'The right-hand edge of the rectangle appears to divide the top of the square into halves, and the top of the square similarly divides the right-hand edge of the rectangle into halves. I

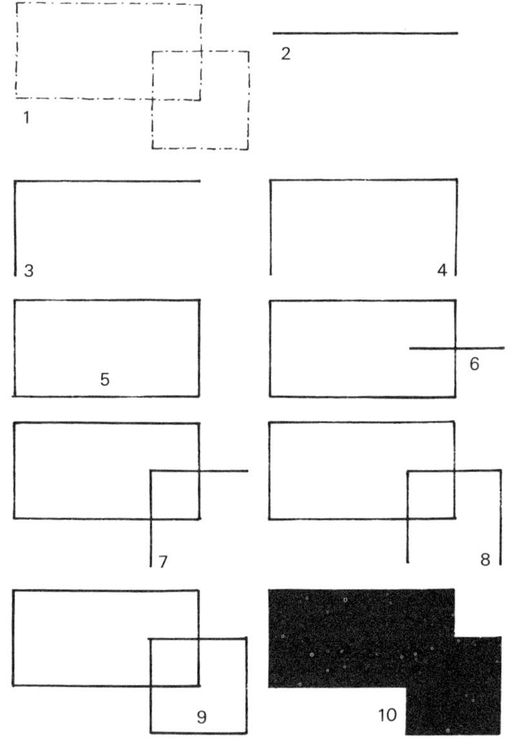

will draw the top of the square so, divided and dividing' (6). 'I will now complete the square, being careful to keep the edges parallel and lengths correct' (7), (8) and (9). 'Now I will block the shape in' (10). It is much less complicated to do than it sounds in words!

There are other ways of doing it, but that basically is how we measure with our eyes. Each line or point, each curve and mark is checked against others until the drawn shape is correct. Do not be afraid of making mistakes or of redrawing lines. It is necessary to work things out and even the greatest masters of drawing made 'mistakes'.

Learn also to measure angles approximately. This will help with the drawing of roofs, spires, trees, cranes and everything else where one line grows from another.

Learn to see whether a shape 'fits' into a basic geometric shape, or whether it can be divided up to fit into basic geometric shapes. To measure angles and 'fit' shapes it is necessary to keep an imaginary plumb line 'in front of the eyes', or use background verticals, to check uprightness. A real plumb line can be used if you wish, and the frame already mentioned is useful again here.

Look for lines which flow from one part of a shape to another. Look for lines which are parallel. Look for lines which converge on the same point. Some of these will be seen in the marked photograph of the pony's skull. Seeing such lines will help a great deal as a drawing is laid out and progresses. In the early stages, draw them in continuously. As expertise grows it is increasingly easy to 'jump' over spaces with them. Practise measuring, and finding 'flow' lines, by drawing shapes like an open pair of scissors, an egg whisk, a friend or the front of your house. Measuring can also be done, without actually drawing, as we go about the place where we live. Say

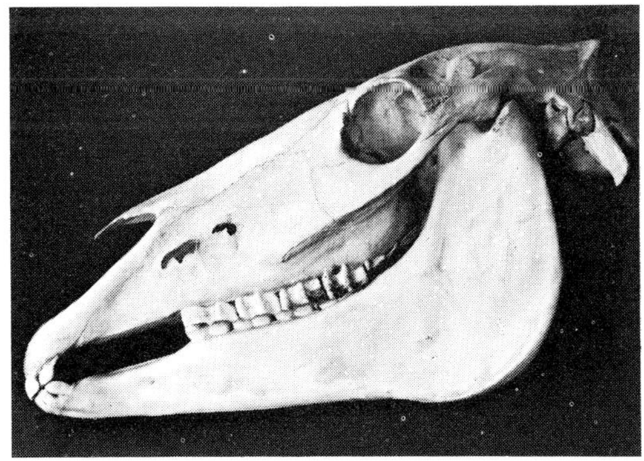

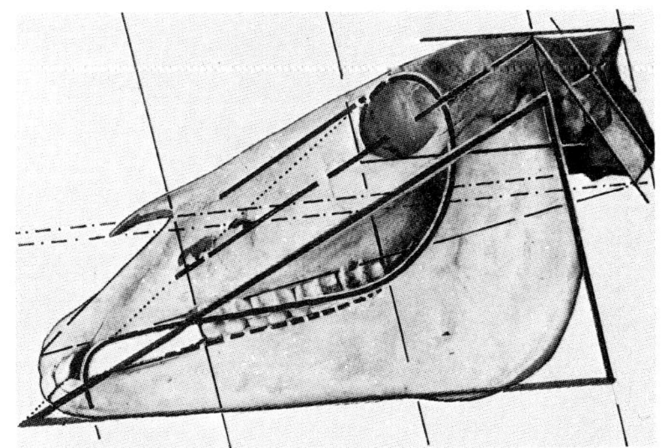

to yourself 'That large building is four times as high and three times as wide as that small house. That tree is an isosceles triangle twice as high as the width of its base.' And so on. It is quite surprising how quickly measuring can be done during an actual drawing when it has become a habit. And you will be able to choose just how accurate you want your drawings to be.

If estimating is found to be too difficult at the beginning, try looking through a frame divided with one or two threads parallel to the edges. Or hold a pencil (or brush) at arm's length. The arm must be kept straight out so that there is a constant base for measurement. The pencil must normally be kept vertical or horizontal depending on the direction in which the measuring is to be done and it is necessary to close one eye. This is essential to give monocular vision and 'flatten' things out. Let us imagine that you want to know how many times higher something is than it is wide. Line up the point of the pencil with one side edge of the object, holding the pencil horizontal. Move the thumb along the pencil and mark the other edge with the thumbnail. Keep it there! Turn the pencil to the vertical position and, using the thumbnail-marked width as a unit, space it off down the height.

Parts of objects can be used as units in the same way—a head for a figure as already mentioned. Spaces can be measured as well, and need to be, in a complicated shape.

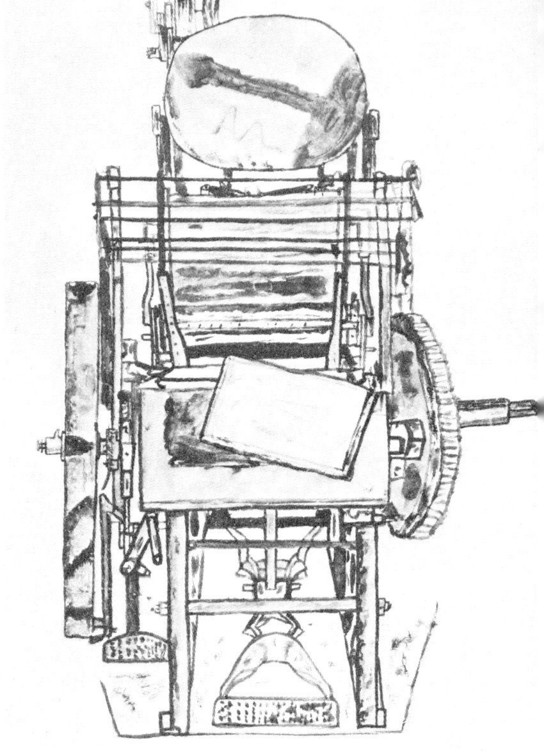

Drawings like those opposite are good practice in measuring. Distances are estimated as the lines are drawn—the same, twice as much, and so on. Producing such designs makes drawing from seen objects like the printing press above much easier.

58

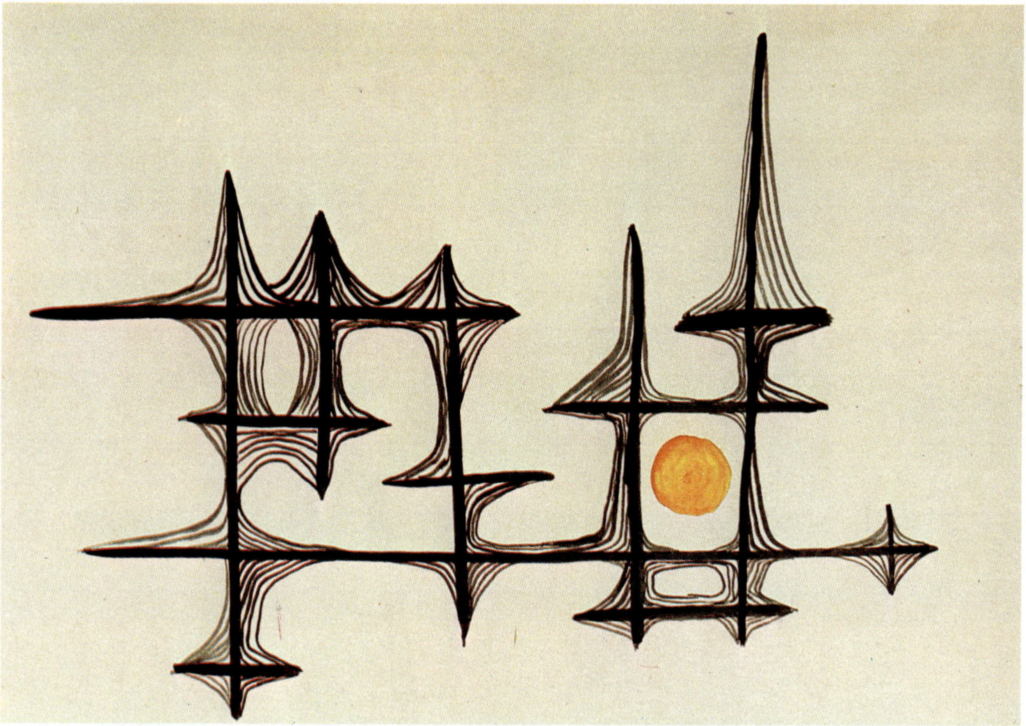

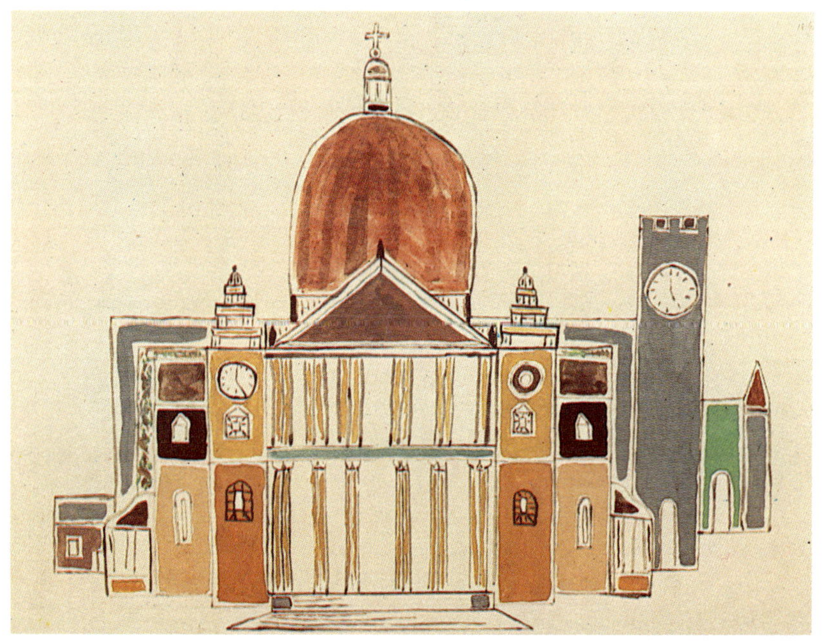

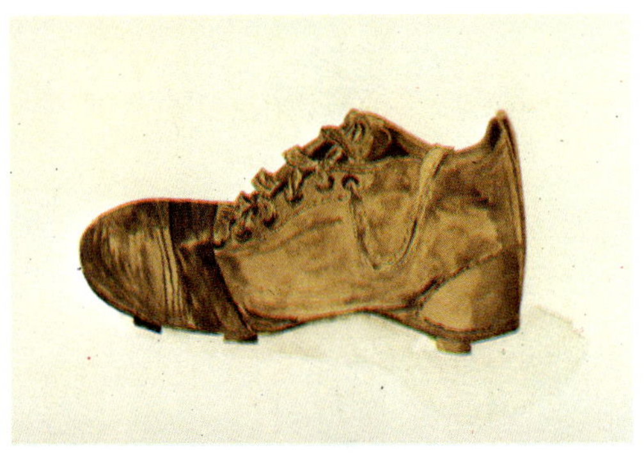

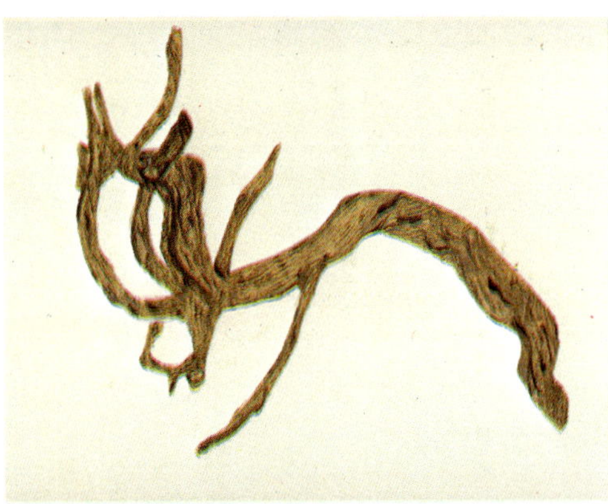

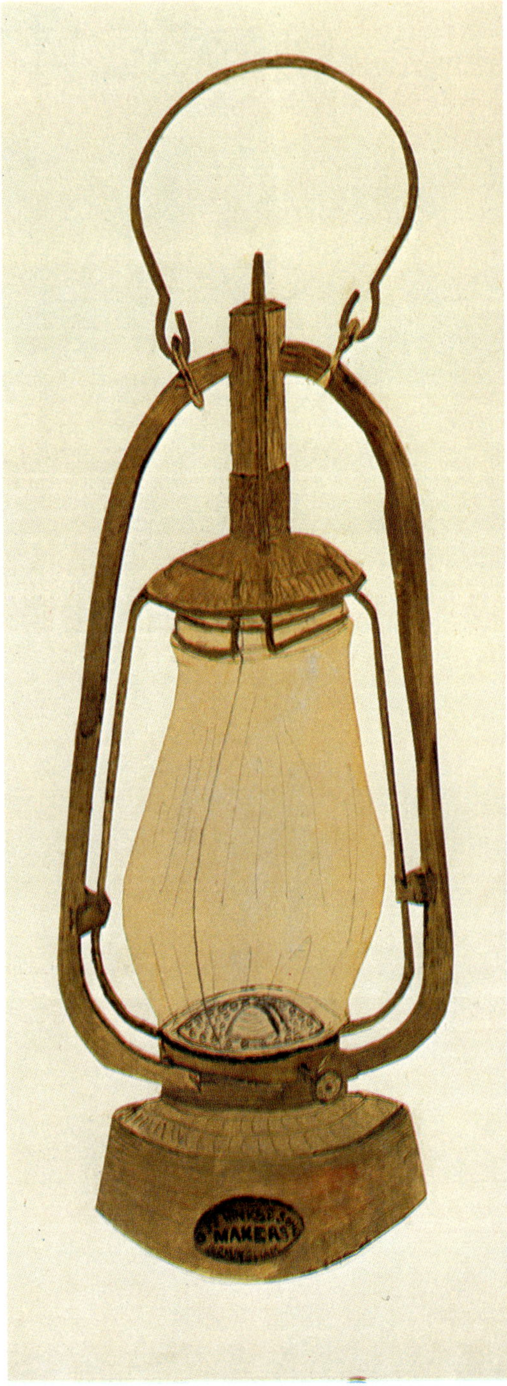

It is possible to achieve an 'instant' darker shape against a lighter background, by cutting the shape of the object from toned or coloured paper. These drawings began on brown paper. The broad character of the shape was drawn on the darker paper and the shape cut out. It was then stuck on to the lighter paper, and the drawing finished with more information. Sometimes, when shapes are 'being difficult', this is a good way to overcome the difficulty. It is also a very easy way to begin drawing a symmetrical object—by folding and cutting half of the shape using the fold as the centre line.

# Drawing is making forms

When the word form is used in drawing, it has several meanings, like the word atmosphere. Atmosphere is the air coverage of the Earth, and its character and content are determined by scientific method. Atmosphere is also what any sensitive person will 'feel' on going into a room full of people—it will feel friendly or otherwise. Even empty places like ruins have this sort of atmosphere, and may feel creepy, or make the fertile imagination expand with the grandeur of events long ago. A work of art is said to have form and, in the same way, this includes the 'feeling' which it has and conveys to the observer. Every good drawing has this kind of form, but for present purposes, form means the volume, the solidity, the three-dimensional structure of things revealed by light. Something which is flat, or something solid seen in silhouette, has shape. Something which has length, width and depth has form. Its solidity, or the space it encloses, will be shown by the light which falls upon it. This will give it what most people call light and shade, or variation in tone around its volume.

**Tone**

Tone in drawing is the scale of grey from white to black, or from light to dark. Tone is essential in all drawing, but there is a difference between light and dark, and light and shade. All the drawings in this book have light and dark or it would not be possible to see them. Some only have light and shade.

In all drawings illusions are created, rather as a conjurer does, but in drawing form—making a drawing with volume— it is necessary to create a particularly clever illusion. We have to make something look solid on a surface which is flat. This has been called stereoscopic illusionism.

Tone, with its range of lights and darks and in-between greys, is essential in creating this illusion of solidity. We have to learn to make even areas of tone. Charcoal, chalk and soft pencils are easiest for this, but exciting preliminary work can be done with torn newspaper. If a page of a newspaper is studied it will be observed that it is a pattern of light and dark. Tearing out patches of these tones and using them to build up drawings is easy and very effective. The idea of 'drawing' by cutting and tearing paper and pasting the shapes together is already familiar. Here are drawings of an iris and a cat done in this way. This method is suitable for many other subjects—even landscape—and can lead to fine tone control.

With charcoal, chalk and pencil, practise drawing very lightly to very heavily, first of all just producing squares or patches of different tones, and later making strips which gradually darken from one end to the other as the medium is pressed on more heavily. Start by hatching the lines in all directions, but try eventually to keep all the lines moving more or less in the same direction. The tone will then be varied by spacing and pressure—and of course by choice of medium: black chalk will make darker tones than a hard pencil.

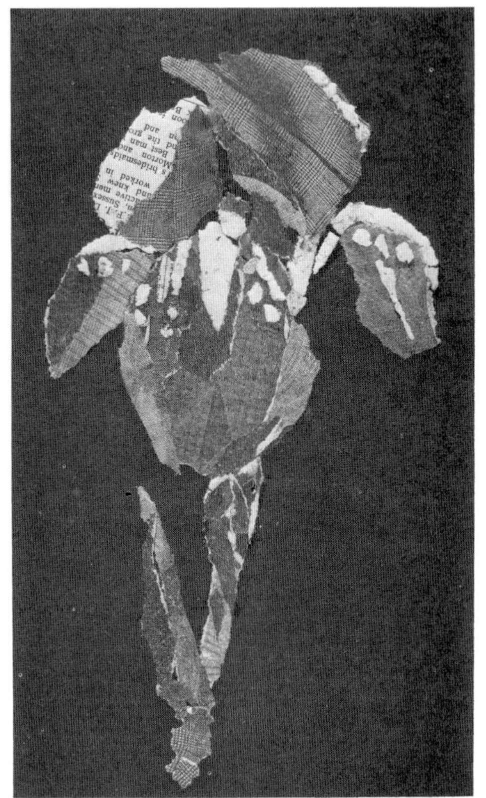

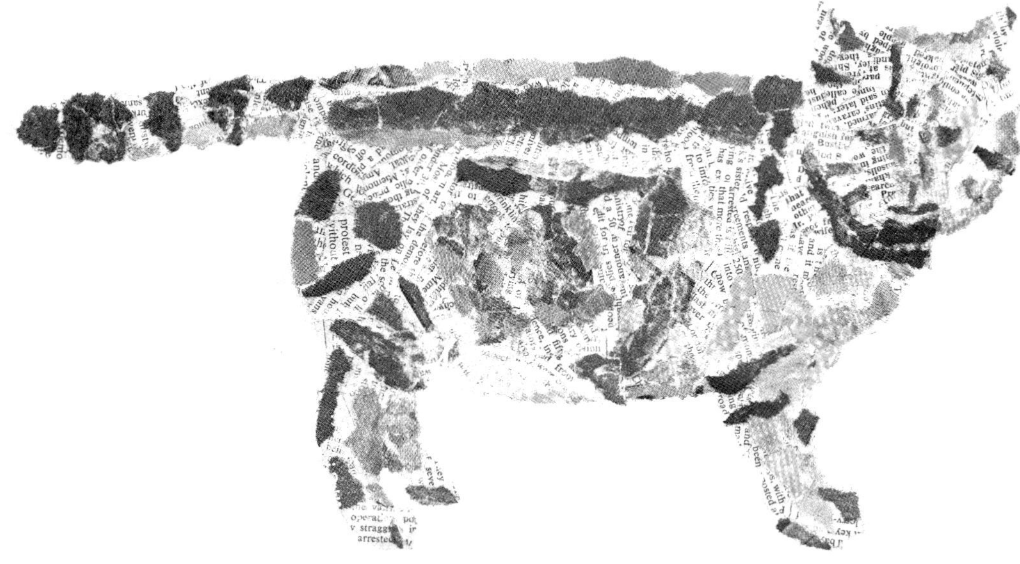

Now let us see how things are made to look solid with tone. Actually, most people do not want to bother about drawing volume at first. Indeed the Japanese hardly ever make things look solid and they produce superb drawings. But in the western world there is a tradition of making things look solid and so it is as well to know how to do it. There will be occasions when it will be necessary to make something look solid to give more information about it. The left-hand drawing below of an imaginary machine might be of a flat wire frame-work. The other drawing, where tone has been added, and varied round the shapes, shows that it is a three-dimensional form whose solidity is revealed by light. If a cast shadow were added, the illusion would be complete, but shadows are a bit tricky, being related in shape to the form which casts them, the angle of light and the shape upon which they fall. At this stage they can be left, unless something is being drawn from life and the shadows are clear.

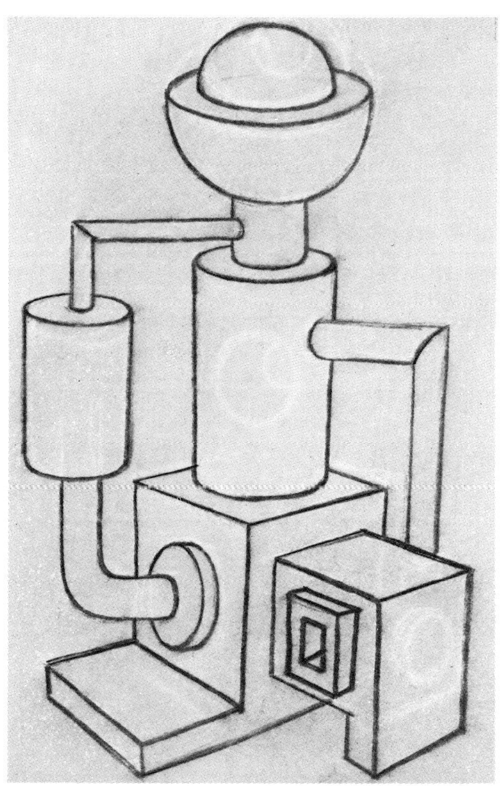

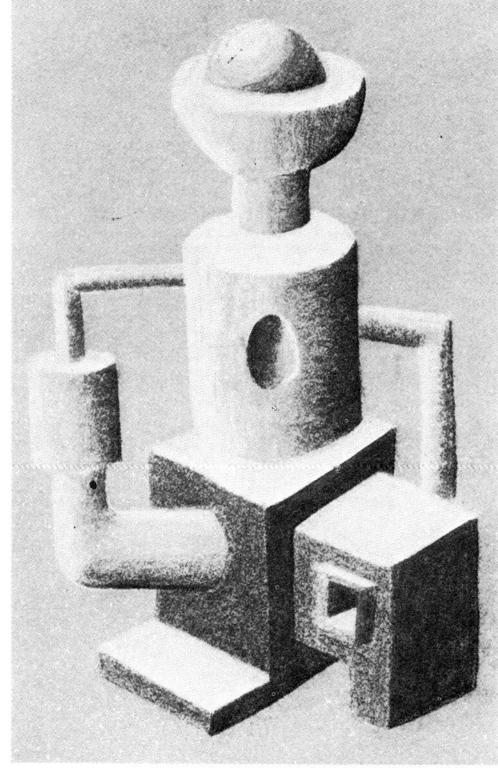

## Making things solid

See now how easy it is to create the illusion of three-dimensions. Look at this series of seven drawings which were drawn on grey paper with a pointed brush and paint. The first is a flat pattern of shapes drawn carefully in relationship to each other, as is now familiar. In the second drawing, vertical lines have been added and it shows the first and simplest convention for showing three-dimensions. But the second drawing might still be of a flat wire framework. The third drawing adds an area of solid dark tone, and it is now easier to accept that these are solid objects. It has been assumed that light is falling from the left, which is another convention, and the tone is black to suggest deep shade. The fourth drawing shows a fairly satisfactory illusion created with line and solid—the lines representing an in-between grey tone. In drawing five there is a rather different approach. Now only a few lines are necessary, because white has been introduced for the lightest planes. The tone of the paper is now the intermediate between white and black—lightest and darkest—and it is only this which requires to be defined with line. In drawing six all lines have disappeared with the total use of tones— white, grey and black. The seventh drawing shows how powerfully the illusion is created with the use of internal spaces as well. Note the logical distribution of the toned areas. It is no more difficult than that. Try this, either making separate drawings or one drawing built up stage by stage. If you enjoy giving imagination a free rein, make a drawing of a space city, or an aerial view of a ruined ancient metropolis. Colour can, of course, be used, but keep to one colour, with black and white for mixing the various tones.

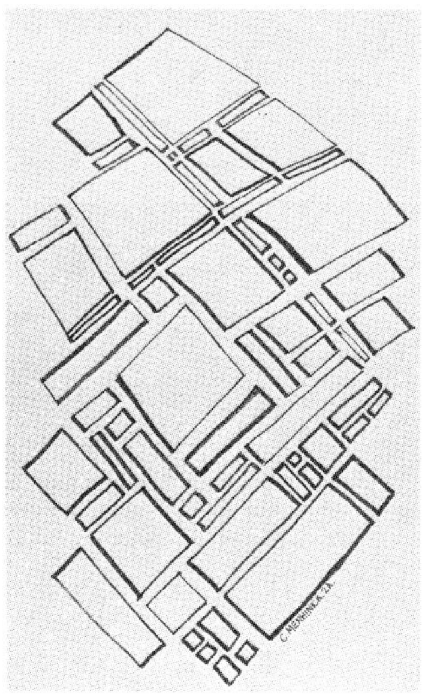
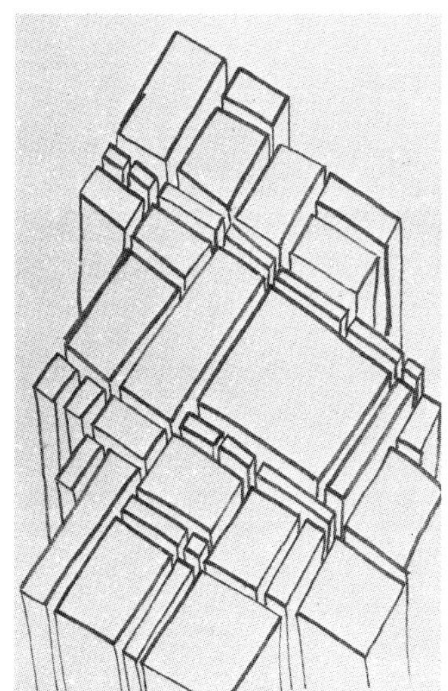
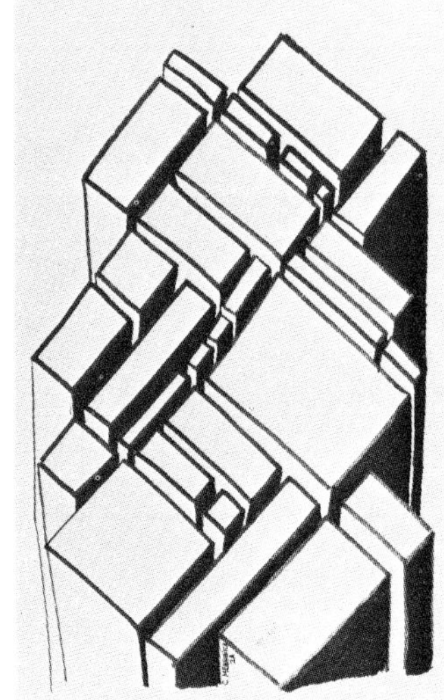

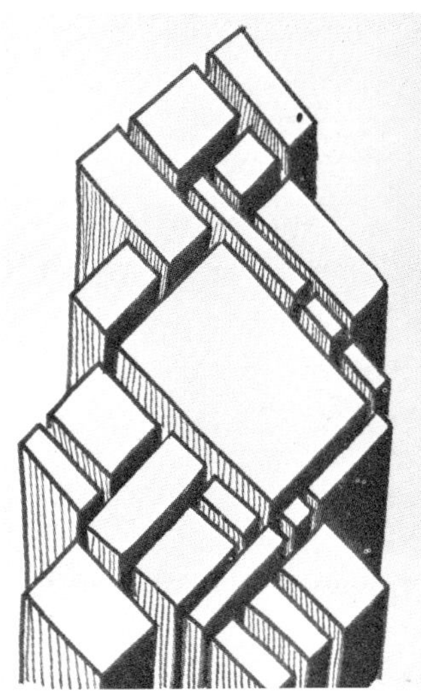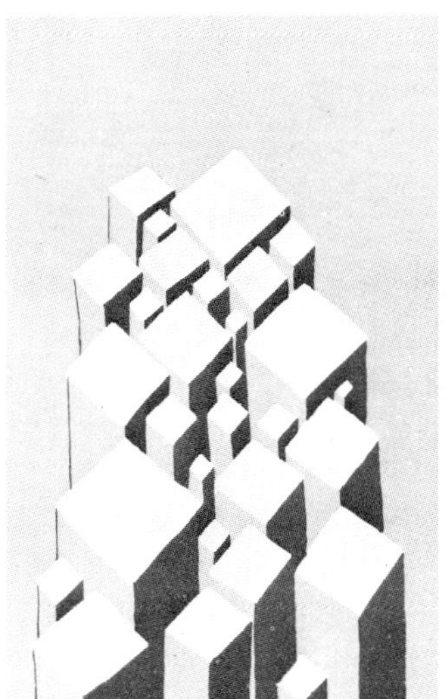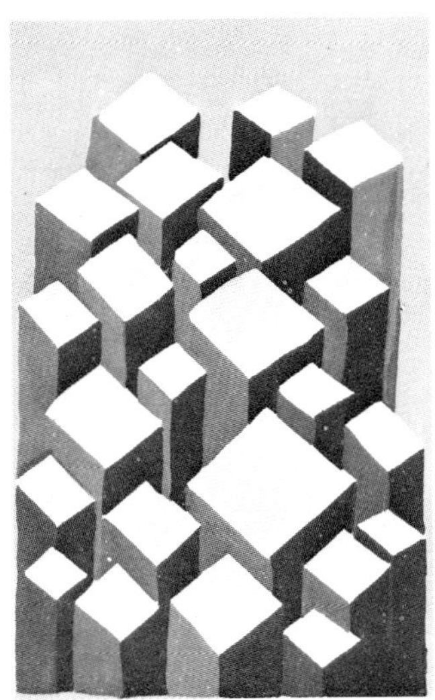

In these experiments, patches of tone have been made, controlled so that they are as dark or as light as required. The grading of tone from light to dark by increasing pressure, and building up lines, will have been mastered. It will have been seen how carefully distributed tone produces the illusion of solidity. Now consider objects with curved surfaces. It is easiest to work with white chalk and charcoal on a grey paper about halfway between white and black in tone. This fixes the middle, and the extremes of the range from light to dark: the white chalk will make the light areas, the charcoal the dark areas, and both will shade away into the middle grey of the paper.

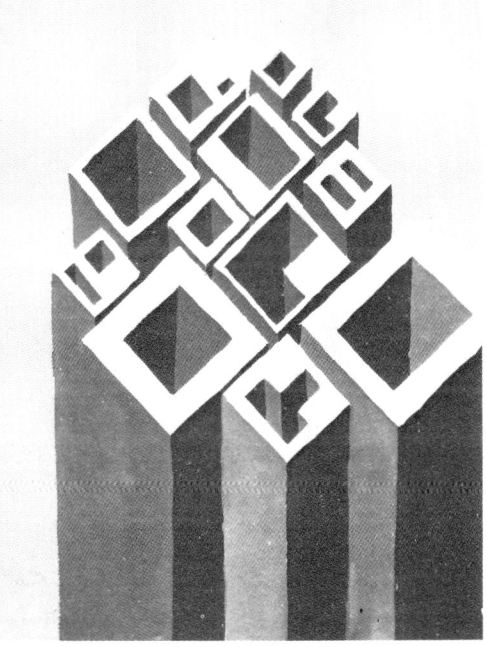

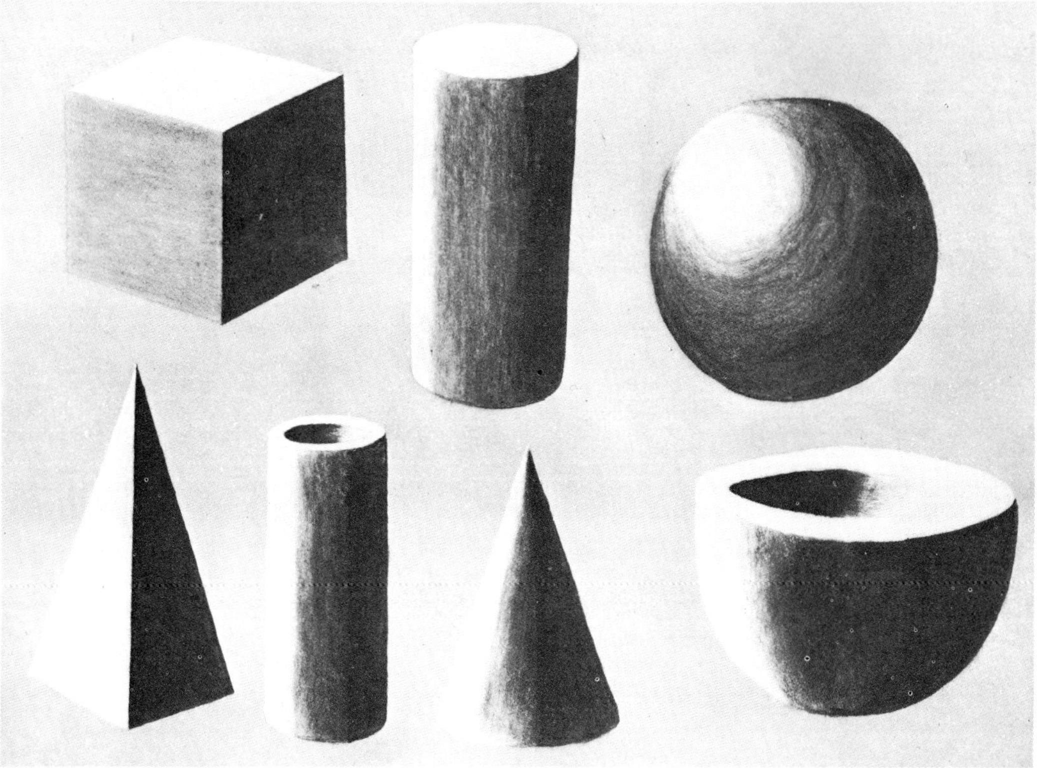

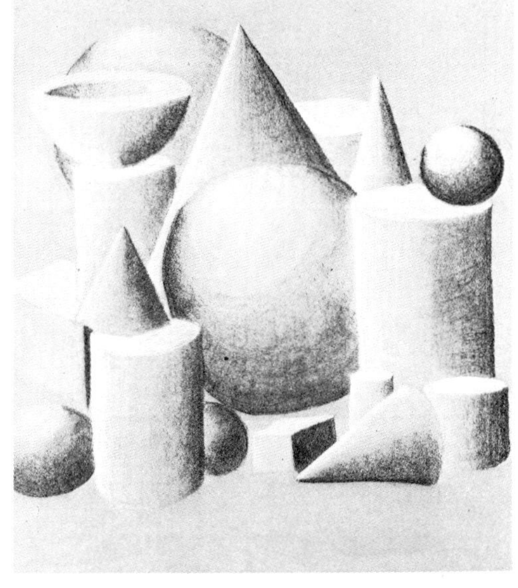

Draw some simple solids singly or grouped, like those on this page. Do this from memory because reflections and variable light on 'seen' objects can be confusing until the basic idea is mastered. Build up the 'unseen' forms working without an outline. If you must use an outline as a beginning, draw it very lightly, and 'lose' it, because outlines flatten tone drawings. A crisper drawing will be produced if the chalk and the charcoal are kept apart as in the grouped solids, but it is the illusion of solidity which matters. Think of light falling away around the shape of the object so that it becomes gradually darker.

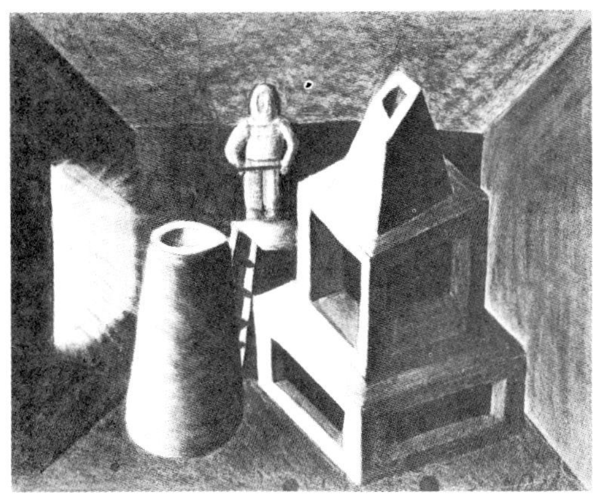

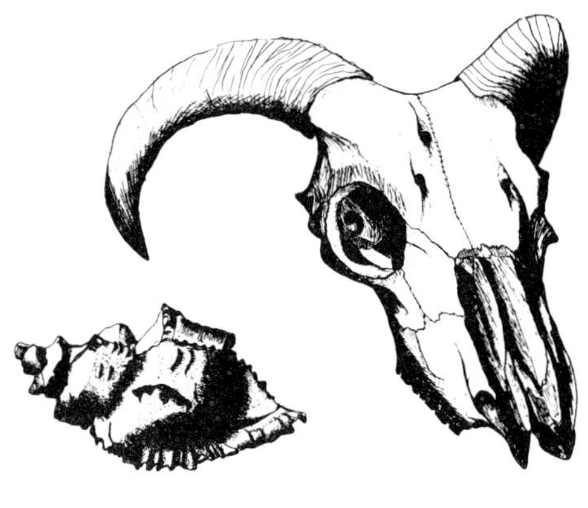

ing press use ideas already considered, but notice how light areas are left untouched. Texture produces tone! Once again a choice must be made.

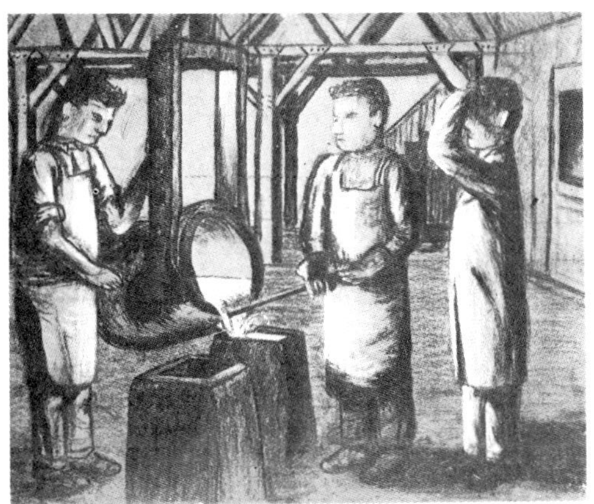

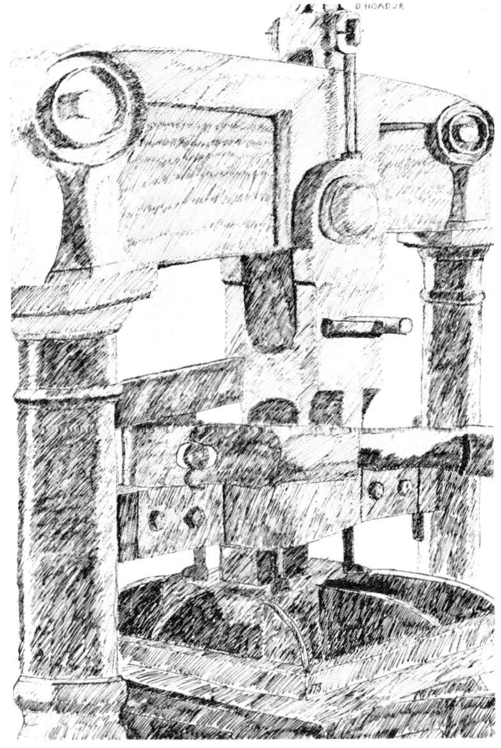

It is helpful to make this your 'doodling' subject for a time—solids from pencil, ballpoint or pen.

Develop pictures using solids and the fall of light as themes, like the foundry drawings above. Take up your pen again, drawing objects which can be seen, keeping all the principles in mind as objects are drawn from observation. These drawings of skull, shell and print-

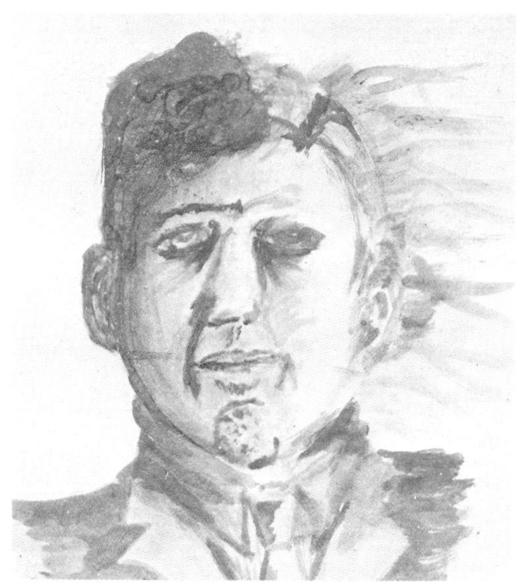

People are rather more complicated solid shapes, but they are not difficult to draw as volumes if the simple geometric shapes—sphere, cylinder, cone—are kept in mind. Some artists have even reduced people to these shapes, and this might be done sometimes for amusement and profit. Emphasize dark and light sides and keep them continuous. The portrait on the left was painted. With paint, remember that more water or white will make tones lighter—black the reverse. The chalk and charcoal drawing below shows space as well as volume because the volumes are placed in depth.

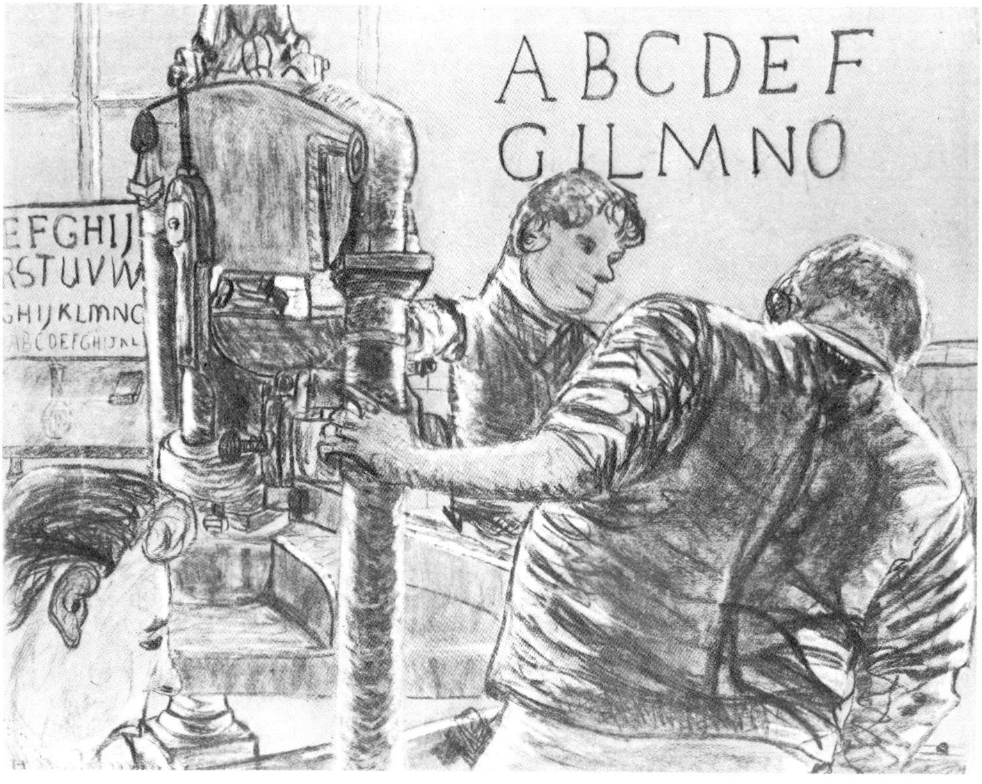

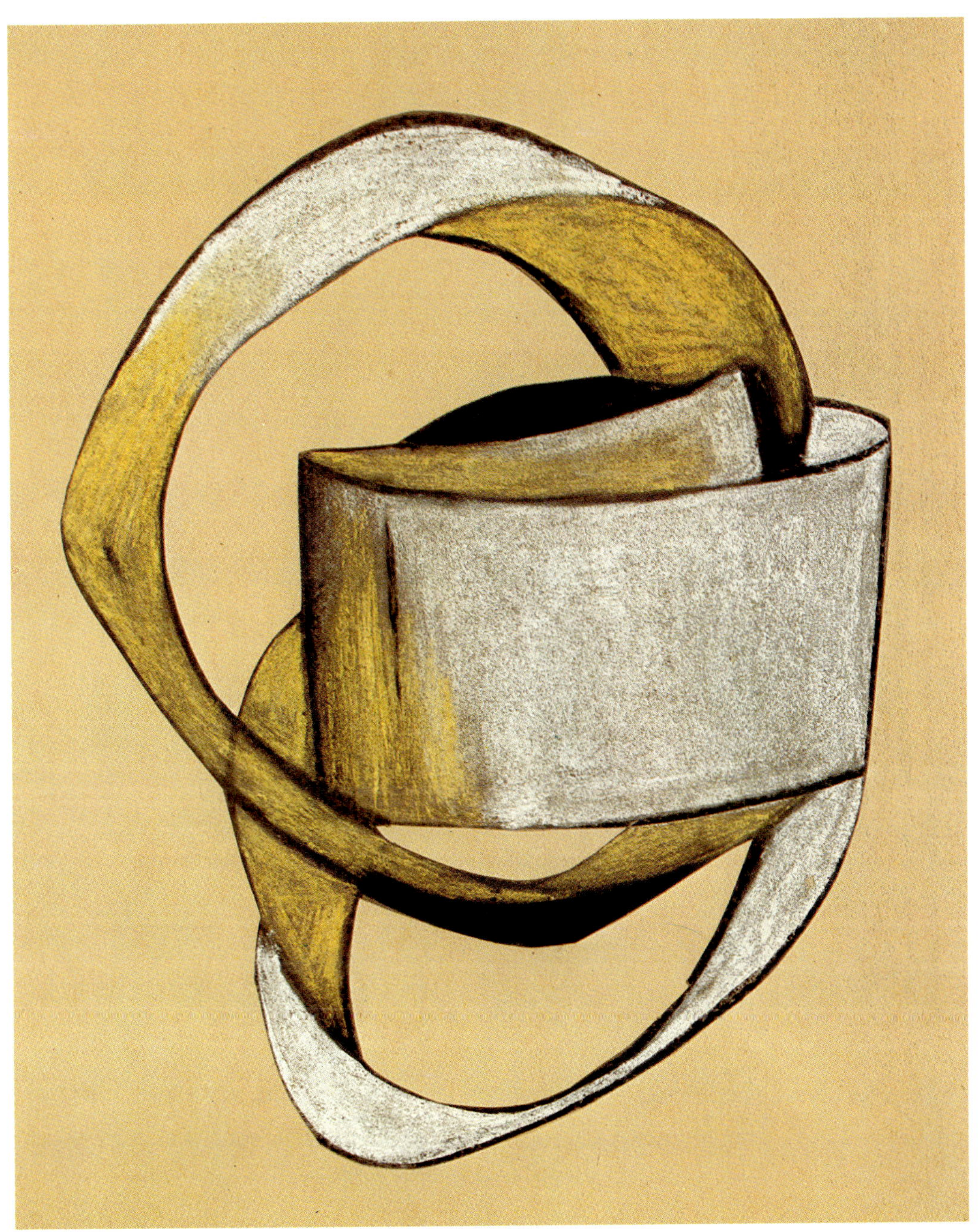

A curl of paper is a splendid abstract form, and is a good subject for studying curved surfaces.

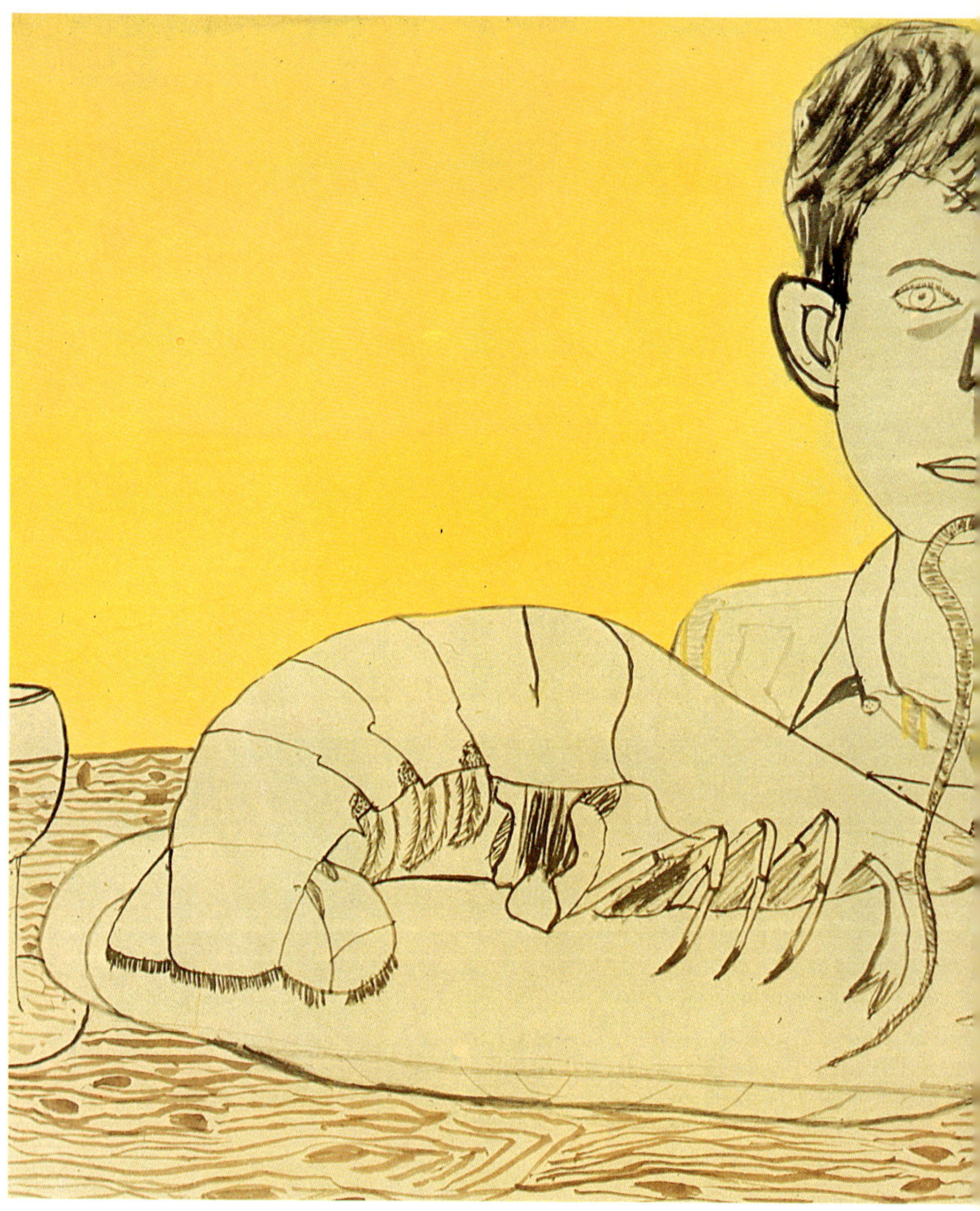

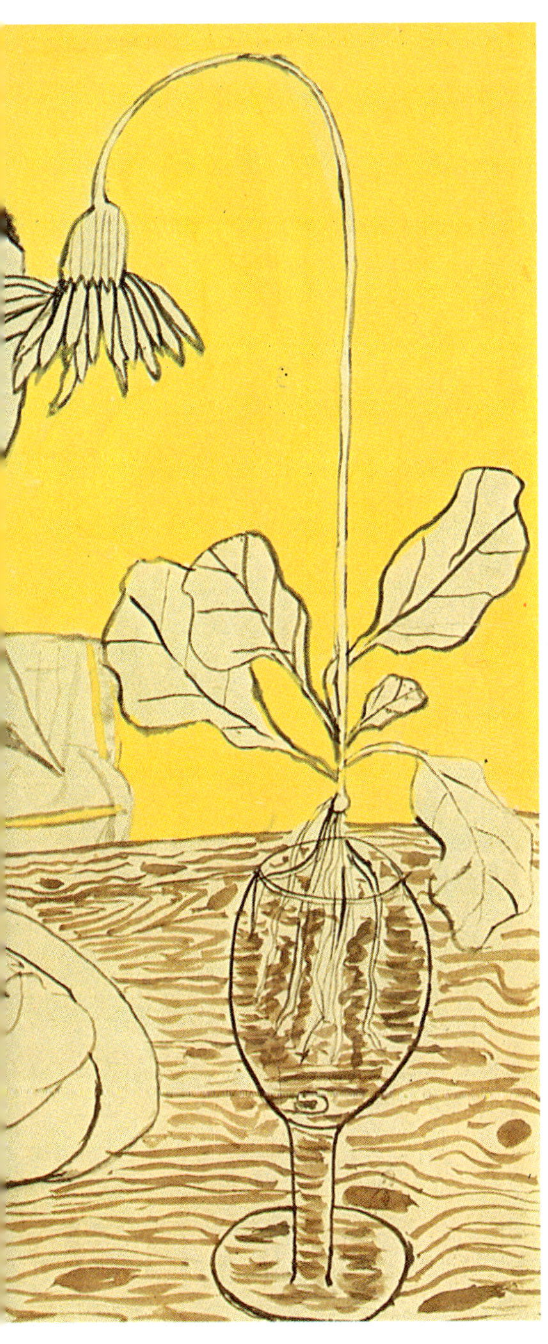

Volumes stand in space, and the creation of the illusion of space is important in many drawings. How do we know that one object is in front of another? If it is understood that they are physically the same size, then we learn by experience that the object which is seen larger is closer. If one object is partly obscured by overlapping, we know that one is behind the other. When objects are further away they become lighter in tone, the contrast between light and dark grows less, colour becomes fainter and changes in the extreme distance to grey-blue. All this can be seen particularly clearly on a misty day, and all these points can be used in drawing to create space.

Most important is the difference in size or scale. This is perhaps most effectively noticed in a cinema or theatre when someone's head is in front of you! The drawing on the left, which does not attempt to describe volume, uses the difference in scale to suggest depth. The lobster is not a prize-winner—it is just closer. There are experiments in observation which will demonstrate this clearly. One is to stand behind goalposts. It will be seen that those at the far end are very small, and fit into the corner of those which are closer. The observation of people at different distances is even more interesting. It is helpful to close one eye. This is part of the complicated study of perspective. For now, look hard and relate things carefully to one another.

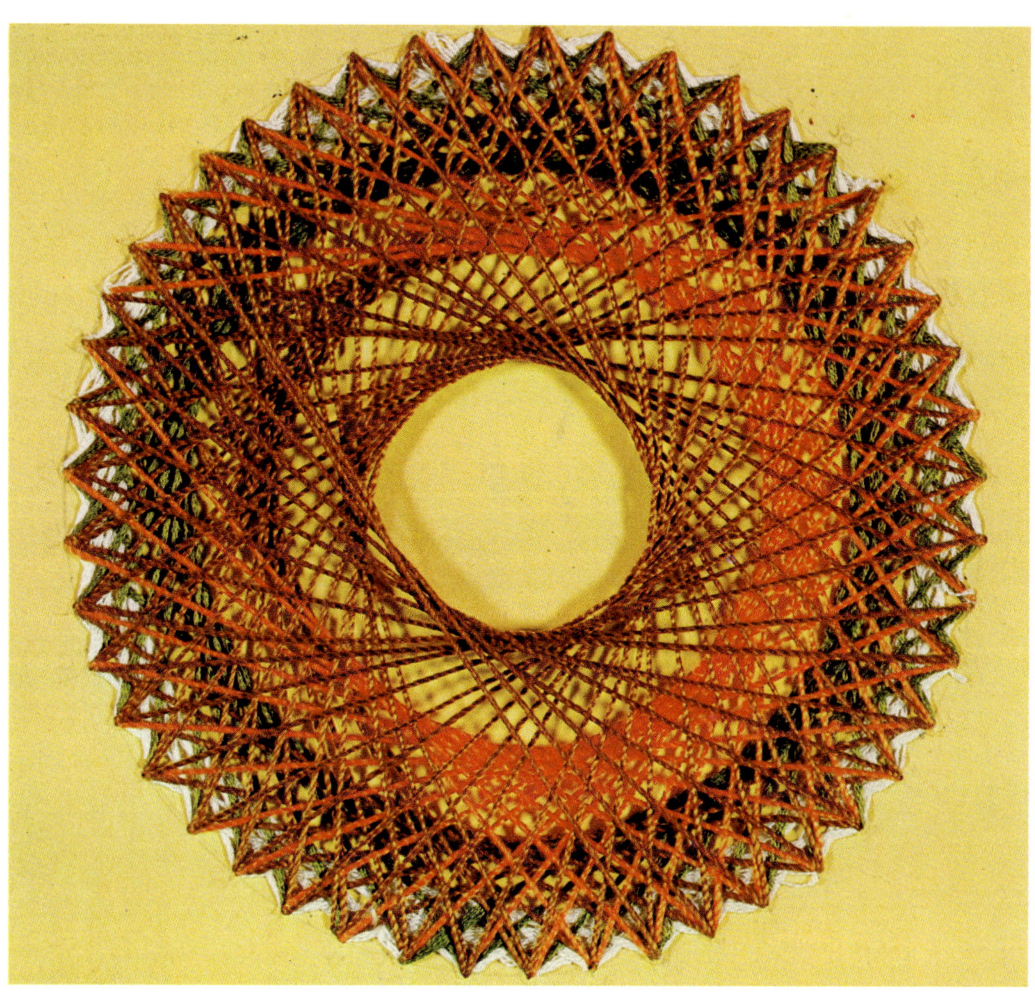

This 'drawing', worked in thread while doing mathematics, reminds us that many materials may be used for drawing, and that drawing is produced for many reasons. It will be noticed how the stitching of straight lines produces curves. Interesting patterns are constantly resulting from our actions.

The threads of the design are harmonious in colour. A harmony of colour—or tone—is achieved when one grows naturally from the other—yellow, yellow orange, orange, red and so on. Colour in drawing will be most effective when it is simple.

Nature is our best teacher, and the subtle colours of natural things are those which should be studied, and used.

# Drawing is seeing

Earlier in this book it was said that people who look hardest at things usually draw better than those who do not. It was suggested that they 'see more'. This does not mean that their eyesight is physically better. They just use their eyes to greater effect in conveying information to the mind.

In drawing we use two eyes, but in more than one sense. We have an outward eye which looks at the world, and an inward eye which looks at feelings, memory and imagination. In fine drawing, outward and inward-looking eyes work together. Memory can help a person to see. It can also be a great hindrance if it stores up worn-out childish shapes! One way in which the memory can help is by providing lists of words about things when the images are forgotten. If you want to draw a motor car from memory, how many things can you remember which make up a motor car? For a start, think of the wheels, and do not forget the pattern of the tread, or the caps on the valves. It will be a very long list, and a drawing including everything on it would give a great deal of information. It might

not look like any particular motor car— for this to happen the shapes must be in the right proportion and relationship. But it would say a lot about motor cars. Gradually memory will store up more and more images, and these will help in seeing things more clearly, provided the images are kept fresh. Try looking at a complicated object—perhaps a painting by a great artist—for a while each day, and notice how your eyes tell you more and more about it as the days pass. It is a rewarding exercise to write down what is seen.

What does each thing which you see really look like? 'Something like this' is not quite good enough. But, of course, having seen, we *re*present, and a drawing will never look exactly like something seen, because it is made of marks on flat paper, and not solid flesh and blood, or wood, or millions of leaves stirring in the wind. It is like translating words from one language into another. Not exactly the same, but having the same—or more—meaning. In drawing we see, understand and translate. From knowledge, and from choice.

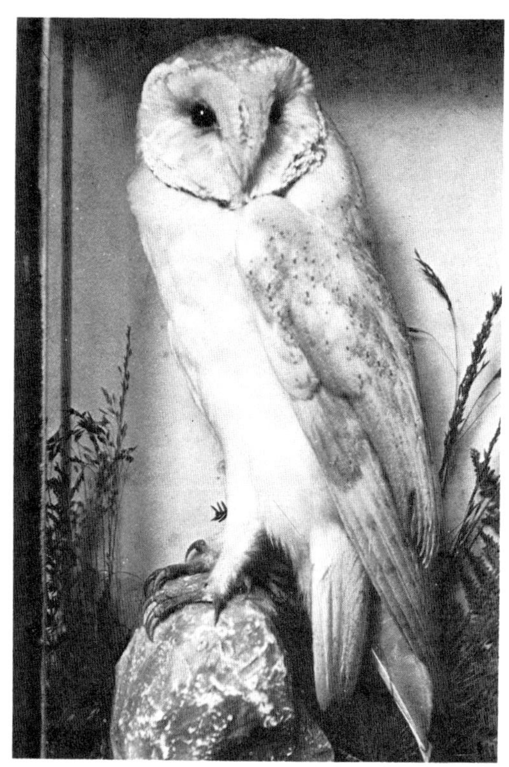 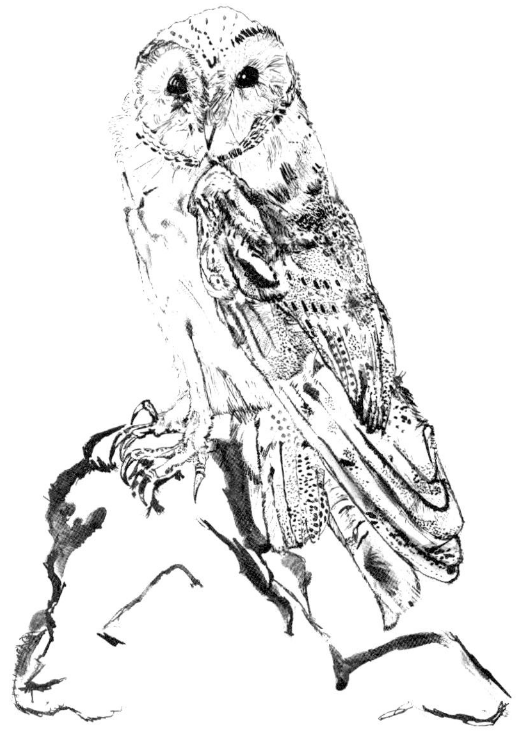

Seeing is a very personal affair. Each of us is unique, and brings to the use of the eyes a personal level of curiosity, interests, character, intelligence, customs and training. An Australian aboriginal sees and draws a kangaroo differently from a European. Drawing—an active result of seeing—is affected by all the things mentioned, but real seeing and fine drawing most needs endless curiosity. If you have this, you will draw well—if not immediately, then after the necessary degree of practice, without which nothing can be done satisfactorily. All people who are very curious about the structure of things draw well—botanists and geographers are typical.

Above is a photograph of a barn owl, and a drawing and two linocuts which the owl inspired. The linocut on page 5 is another. The young artist who made the first owl drawing wanted to say something about it, and explore its textures with a pen and ordinary ink which could be rubbed while still wet. The linocut owls were all made after practising, and the artists let their imaginations develop them into pictures with quite different moods. In those above, see how energetic one is, and how calm the other. It will be apparent how these effects were achieved.

Shapes and forms are carried in the

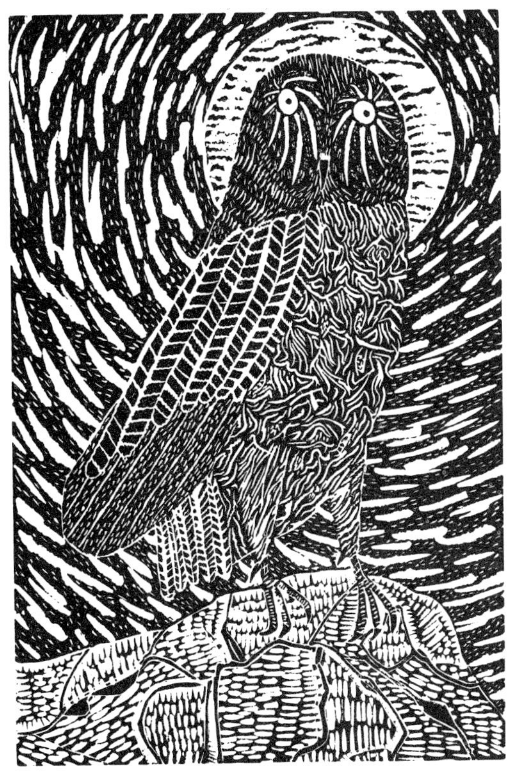

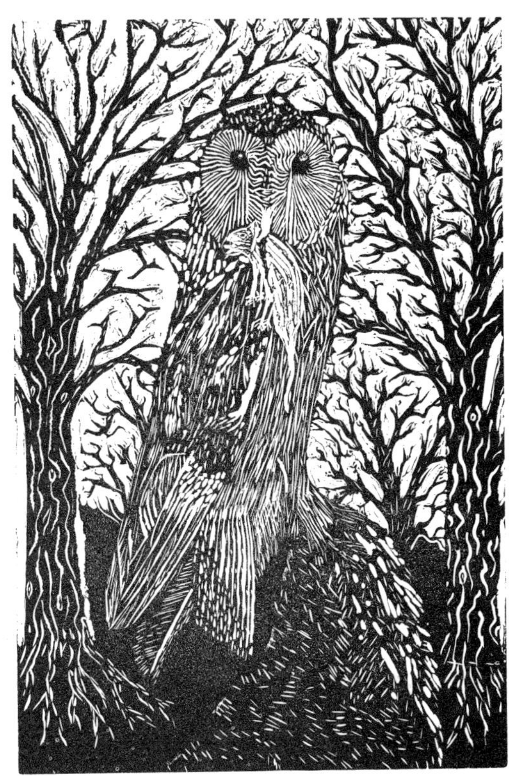

imagination. Apart from their interest as pure forms, a piece of waste cork and a pebble lying on the beach said 'owl' to me and here they are. Collecting shapes like this is rewarding, and if the object is examined seriously as a form as well as letting it say 'owl', or whatever, to us, it will help in the development of a good sense of design.

This is very important for choosing houses and furniture, pottery, glass and

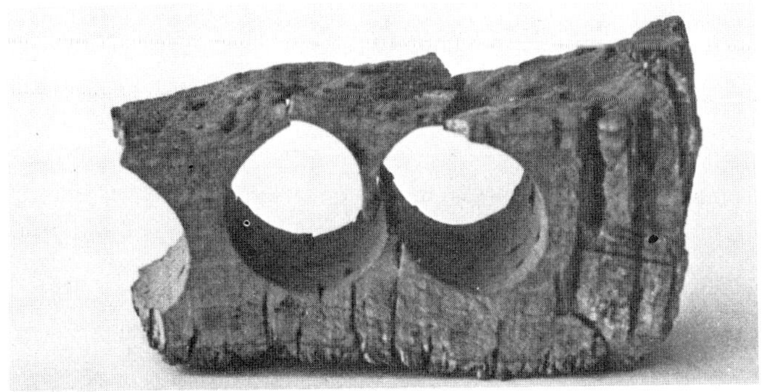

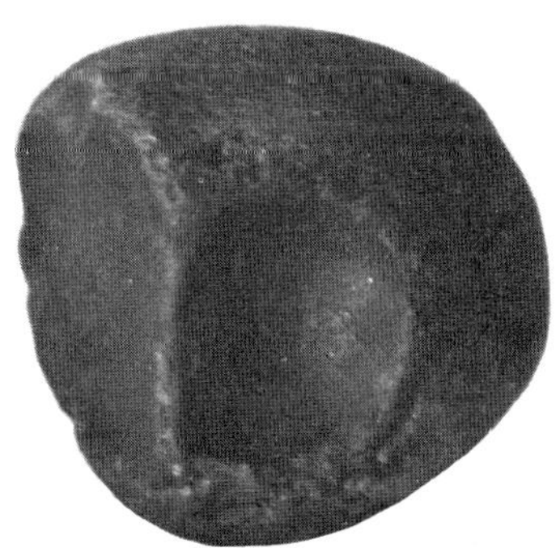

all the objects which we use. A whole town has form. It is an enormous piece of sculpture in which people move about.

Never actually turn natural things into something else. They are beautiful enough in their form and colour, and they do not need to be painted or turned into funny figures. Just let them work on your imagination and help you to see. See and draw with what has been called a 'thinking eye'.

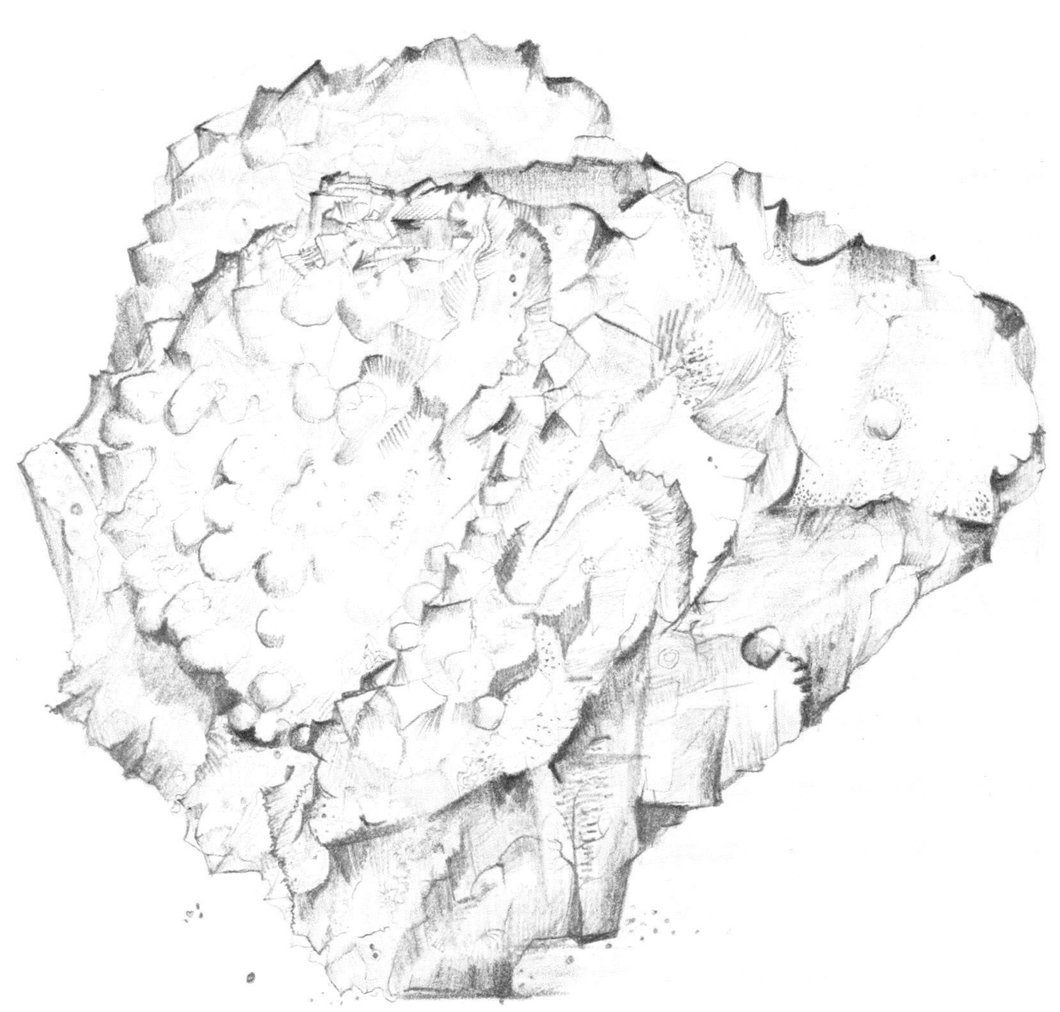

## A few last words . . .

The drawings here and overleaf were made by young people of sixteen or so, and they had spent some years practising and developing their drawing skill.

Words can act as thought-starters, help with information, begin to explain, but undoubtedly the very best way to understand and improve drawing is to draw. And draw. And continue drawing. It does not matter how simple or rough the first drawings you make are. They prove the ability to draw and from then on it is only a matter of improving that natural ability by use. Closer looking, and further attempts to express what is seen, with all the power of technique developing through practice, will produce more interesting and satisfying drawings. Increasingly, your drawings will express your thoughts, ideas, feelings and discoveries as you want them expressed. More skilful fingers will do what the mind says; the constantly probing mind will sort out clearly, and make a choice of the information given by sharp 'thinking eyes'. Drawing will become a rich and wonderful way of thinking and talking both to yourself and to others.

In all your drawing, consider closely what is in your mind or before your eyes and ask: 'What do I want to say about this?' 'What is this drawing for?' Make decisions about the points which are important and those which are not. In carrying out these decisions with the chosen medium something unique will be produced, as personal to you as face or handwriting—your own drawing. You can do it because you are a human being.

Enjoy it!

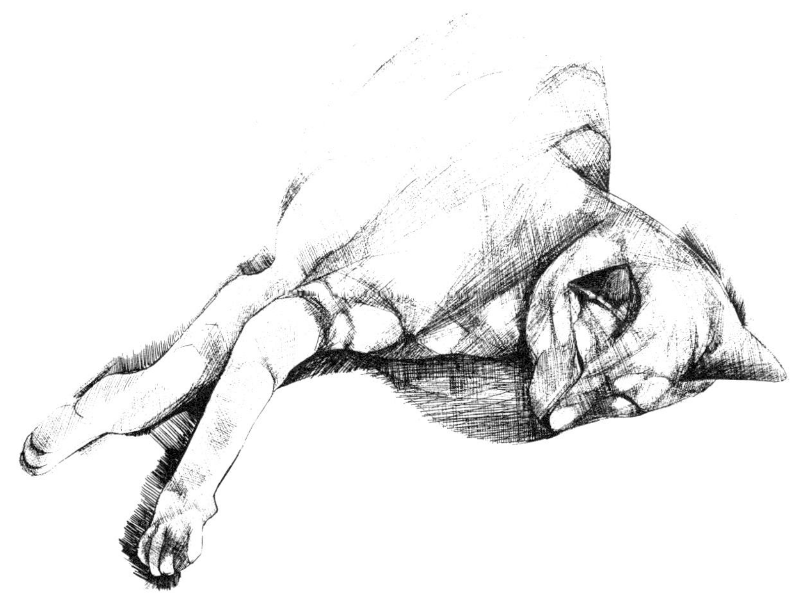

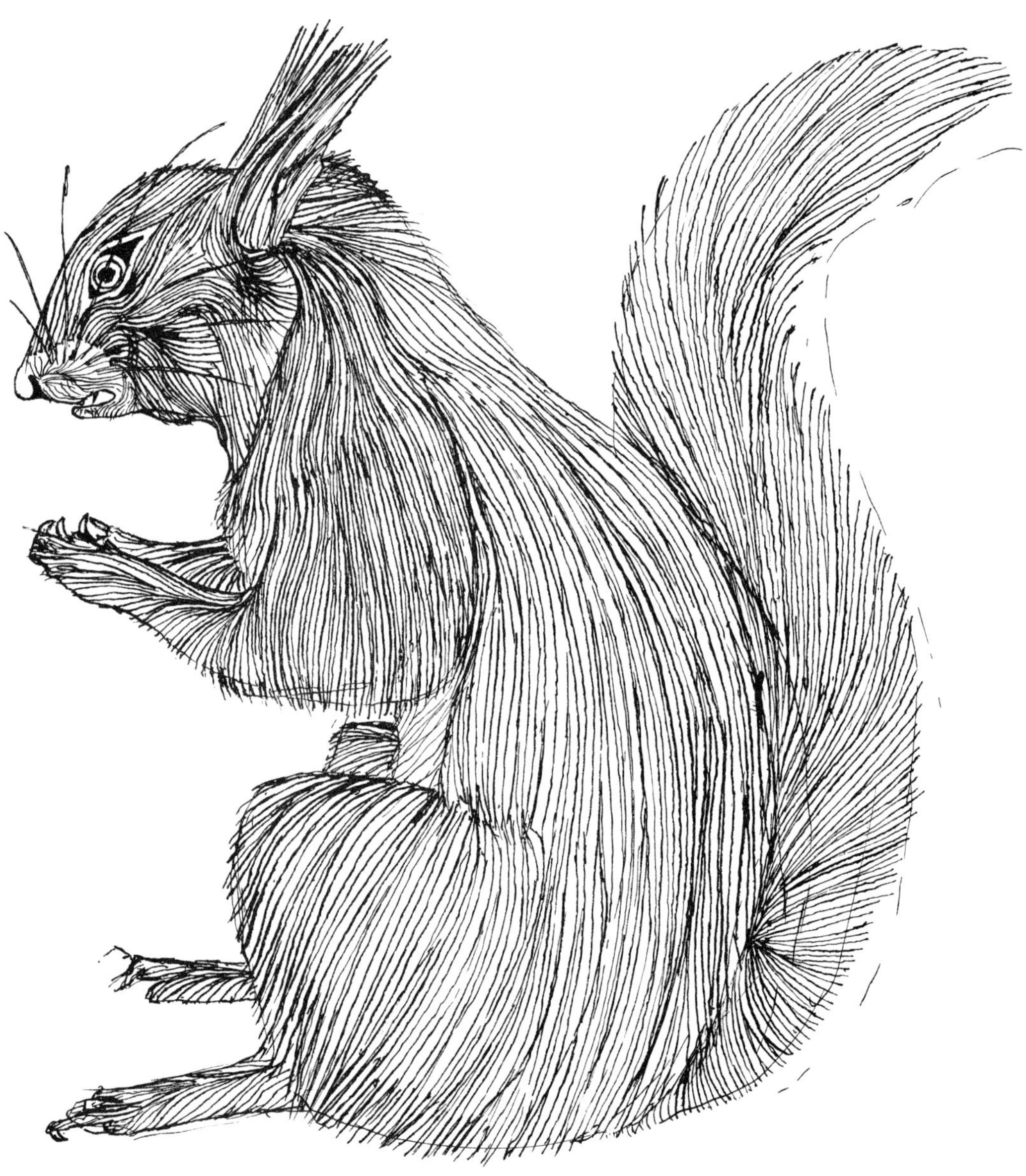

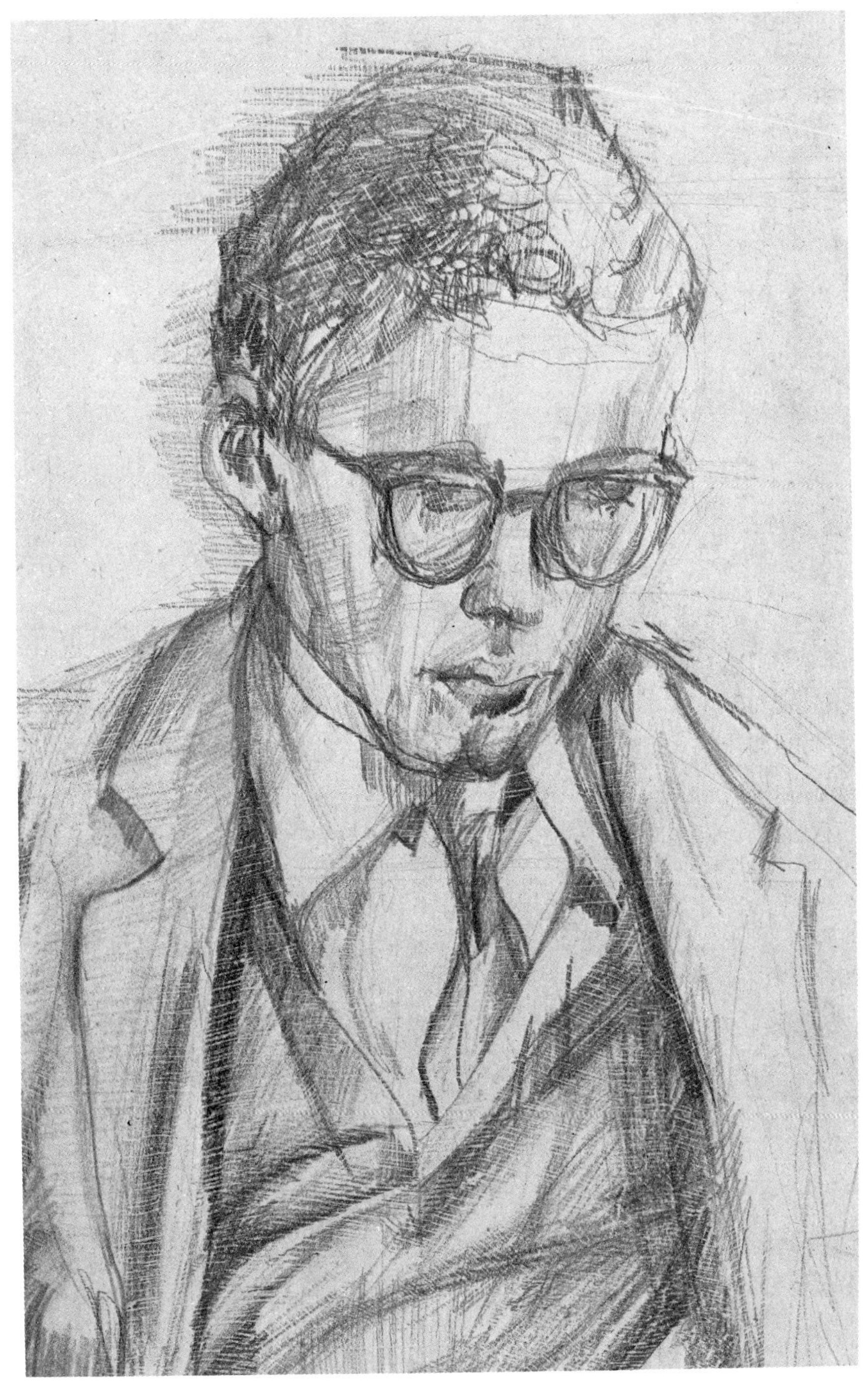

**Other books to read**

*You can draw*, Kenneth Jameson, Studio Vista/Watson Guptill.

*Creative drawing*, Ernst Röttger, Batsford/Van Nostrand Reinhold.

*Learning to see*, Kurt Rowland, Ginn/Van Nostrand Reinhold.

*Drawing with Pencils*, Norman Laliberte and Alex Mogelon, Van Nostrand Reinhold.


**Acknowledgement**

The author pays tribute to the generations of young people who have learnt to draw with him, and with whom he has learnt his trade. He thanks Miss J. Bonner, Miss P. Lennon, Miss B. Pye, Mr D. Lindsay, MA, and Mr A. Smith, who provided children's work for reproduction, and Mr O. Frampton, ATD, who helped with the photography. He remembers with respect and affection past pupils of Cray Valley School, who did many of the drawings in this book, and whose patience and ingenuity never ceased to amaze him.


Published in Great Britain by Evans Brothers Limited, Montague House, Russell Square, London, W.C.1

Published in the United States of America by
Van Nostrand Reinhold Company
A Division of Litton Educational Publishing, Inc.
450 West 33rd Street, New York, N.Y. 10001

Van Nostrand Reinhold Company Regional Offices:
New York   Cincinnati   Chicago   Millbrae   Dallas

Van Nostrand Reinhold Company International Offices:
London   Toronto   Melbourne




Library of Congress Catalog Card Number 72–1860
ISBN 0–442–29172–8

16 15 14 13 12 11 10 9 8 7 6 5 4 3 2 1

Filmset in 'Monophoto' Imprint by Keyspools Ltd, Golborne, Lancashire and printed in Great Britain by C. Tinling & Co. Ltd, London and Prescot
ISBN 0 237 35244 3                         PRA 2948

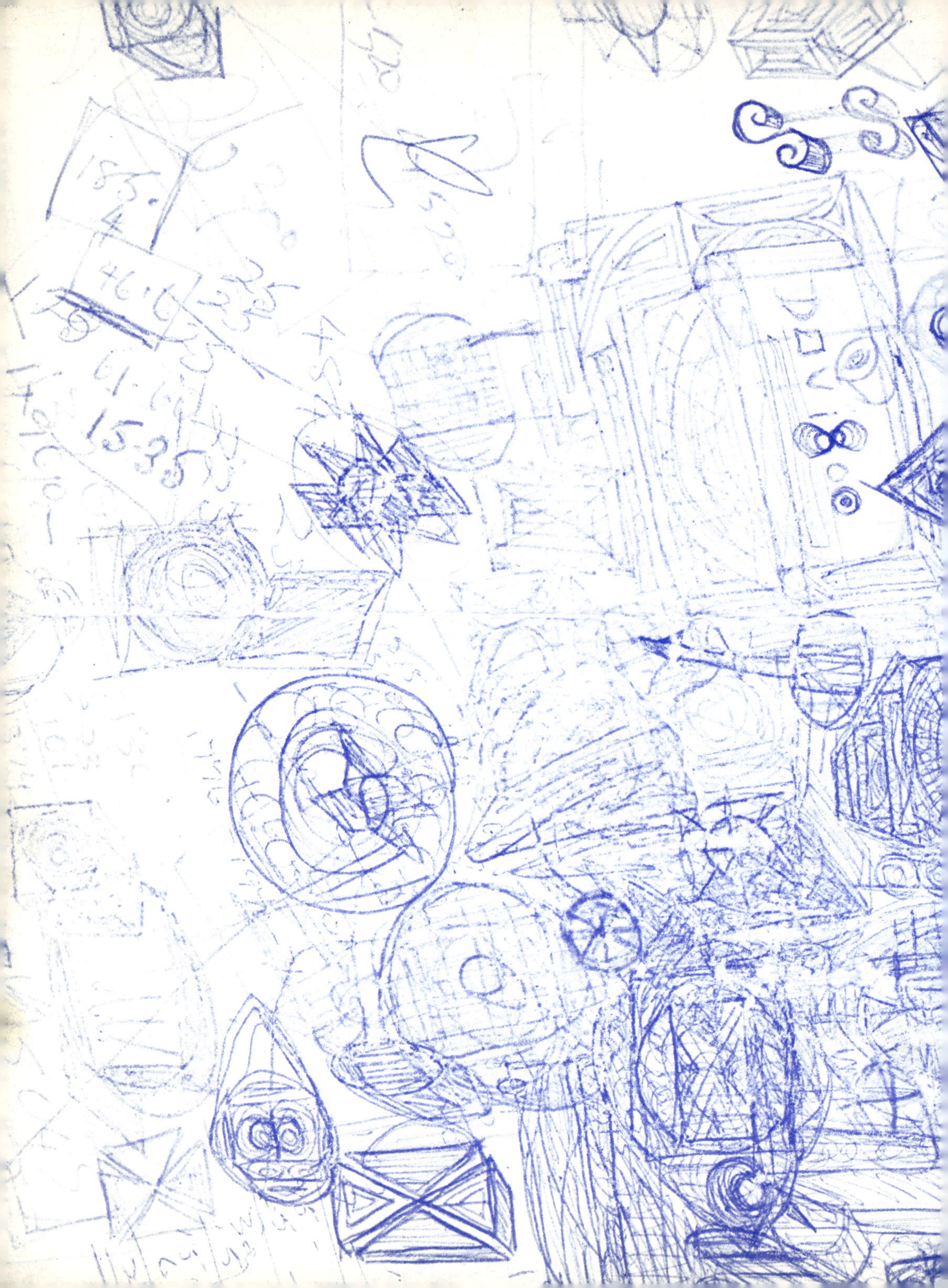